Flip It!

Flip It!

Strategies for the ESL Classroom

Robyn Brinks Lockwood

Stanford University

Foreword by Keith S. Folse

The University of Michigan Press

Ann Arbor

ISBN 978-0-472-03606-6

2017   2016   2015   2014   4   3   2   1

Acknowledgments

I want to acknowledge the authors whose material is included in this book.

Wendy Ashby
Laurie Barton
Susan Benson
Cynthia A. Boardman
Grace Canseco
Mark A. Clarke
Barbara K. Dobson
Christine B. Feak
Keith S. Folse
Kevin B. King
Kathleen Olson
Julia Salehzadeh
Myra Shulman
Sandra Silberstein
John M. Swales
Li-Lee Tunceren
Gladys Valcourt
Linda Wells

I would also like to thank my editor, Kelly Sippell, for her valuable input during the development of this manual and her dedication to publishing materials that can help instructors be even better at what they do in the classroom. Many thanks to all the students who worked diligently and with great participation in my classes; they didn't even know they were in a flipped setting, but it was their progress and development that made me realize flipping could be a good thing for them and me. Thanks, as always, to my parents, both former teachers, for their encouragement to do what is best for the students, and my husband, for listening to all my stories. And, to Darrin and Nathan . . . thank you for your love of learning; you make me love to teach.

To all the teachers who want to try flipping, please do. Good luck! Let me know how it goes!

Foreword

Keith S. Folse, Ph.D.
Professor, TESOL
University of Central Florida

It's a routine of mine that I think most teachers can easily relate to. At the end of my work day, as I drive home after teaching in my university position, I do what I always do: I evaluate how I think the day's classes went, and I try to come up with alternative ways of teaching the material that might be better. This line of inquiry—a type of action research—is at the heart of the scholarship of teaching and learning (Kreber, 2007; Vardi, 2011).

Some 35 years ago, I taught my first ESL class in an intensive program at a large university in my home state of Mississippi. Since then, I've taught many kinds of language courses in very different settings. I've taught ESL at a small college as well as at several large universities in the U.S. I've also taught EFL at military programs (in two countries), an English conversation school with adults and young children, a graduate school in a university, and an intensive English program. In this diverse array of settings and programs, I learned early on that to be a really good teacher, I would have to adjust my instruction according to the type of program and the country where instruction was taking place. Intensive programs are not the same as conversation classes. Teaching adults is not the same as teaching children. Teaching in Saudi Arabia or Malaysia is not the same as in Japan or Kuwait.

In addition to teaching English learners, I also have a great deal of experience training pre-service (future) teachers as well as in-service (current) teachers. Working with future teachers has some overlap with working with current teachers, but there are also many differences that a good teacher trainer considers and uses to adjust the instruction. For example, I've had to develop different activities to use with elementary school teachers, high school teachers, intensive program teachers, or adult education teachers.

Because I believe strongly in the adage that learner needs drive everything in a curriculum, I have adjusted my teaching in all of these cases based on actual learner needs. Some students like a more teacher-centered class, some groups need more attention with reading and writing instead of speaking and listening, and other learners prefer games and activities instead of books and other traditional materials. In most of these cases, however, my adjustments have been related to the **learner**.

More recently, however, I have had to adjust my teaching to the mode of delivery of my instruction. Specifically, I've had to convert my regular face-to-face classes—a retronym that wasn't widely used just ten years ago—to a mixed-mode class where we meet live only every other class. Even with my 35 years of teaching experience in a variety of classrooms and with seasoned curriculum and materials design skills, this transition in instruction delivery—also known as teaching—has been a real challenge. I think the fact that my adjustment is in reaction to something other than the learner is part of my professional confusion here.

While this adjustment in delivery is not exactly the same thing as flipping the classroom, there are many similarities. For starters, moving certain instruction online is a common component in flipping a classroom. In addition, I have to choose which material might be better in a flipped environment. I have to think of how to present the flipped material in that online environment, and I have to think about what will happen after the instruction. Will students have to post a question in a discussion area, which is a common online practice, even if they don't have a real question and wouldn't ask that question in a face-to-face meeting? And how will I provide feedback on whatever I require the students to do in reaction to the flipped material, preferably in a way that does not burden me with extra work—that is, *extra* in the sense that in a live class, I don't give all the students some task immediately after instruction that I then have to collect, mark, and return. Yes, I am familiar with many ways to handle these scenarios, but still, this transition requires more than knowing which buttons to activate for students in an online course. It requires a **major paradigm shift** in not only how the instructor presents the material but also how the student reacts to the material.

In *Flip It!* Robyn Brinks Lockwood explains in clear language with concrete classroom examples what it means to flip an ESL classroom. While many works extol the virtues of flipping a classroom, *Flip It!* is the first book that I've seen that offers strategies with specific examples for different types of ESL or EFL lessons.

For those new to flipping an ESL classroom, Part 1 explains what flipped learning is. Part 2 discusses some of the pros and cons of flipping a classroom, with more emphasis on the benefits for the students as well as the instructor. The remaining two-thirds of this book is filled with strategies in various scenarios, such as flipping with technology, flipping without technology, and flipping with existing materials from the textbook, instructor's manual, or the real world.

What makes this book so different from the many resource volumes in our TESOL field? When considering this question, two answers come to mind immediately: the clear writing and the concrete examples.

Far too many books, supposedly written to help teachers, are written in rather verbose, often intentionally opaque language, as if the author needed to guard the information. *Flip It!* offers explanations written in clear, concise language that everyone can readily understand, a feature that takes on even more importance when readers are tackling a subject that is as new to most teachers as flipping their traditional classrooms.

In addition, the author always includes specific examples from ESL textbooks to illustrate how a classroom could be flipped. In fact, the book includes at least 50 exercises and activities taken from 15 ESL textbooks covering grammar, writing, reading, listening, speaking, and vocabulary. After reading this book, teachers will easily be able to envision how they could flip their own classrooms.

I know that reading this book and weighing the rationale for why certain exercises were or were not suitable for a flipped classroom has given me much food for thought regarding my own teaching situation as I grapple with selecting which material students will cover before coming to class as well as how that material will be presented. I am very grateful for my interaction with this material as I continue to figure out how to teach my new online lessons and courses.

References

Kreber, C. (2007). What's it really all about? The scholarship of teaching and learning as an authentic practice. *International Journal for the Scholarship of Teaching and Learning, 1*(1), article 3.

Vardi, I. (2011). The changing relationship between the scholarship of teaching (and learning) and universities. *Higher Education Research & Development, 30*(1), 1–7.

Contents

Introduction

Why I Flipped

On January 10, 2013, Stanford University's campus newspaper, *The Stanford Daily*, ran a story on the front page titled "Flipped classroom gaining popularity among profs." The author discussed professors at Stanford University who had adopted a flipped classroom teaching style. The article quoted professors who had already adopted the flipped model and discussed how they, for the most part, liked the change. The article continued to say that the model was growing in popularity and that instructors' and students' experiences improved. Instructors felt rejuvenated when they were teaching something they had been teaching for years, and students seemed to prefer this "new" way of teaching. Grant applications for flipped classroom support were submitted to the office of the Vice Provost for Online Learning, and nearly half received partial or full funding.

With flipped classrooms garnering attention and popularity at my own university, I conducted a quick online search and found that flipped classrooms extended well beyond the confines of my own university. I discovered that they were being used across the country in a variety of disciplines; it wasn't something simply being adopted by one instructor at one university, which meant I probably needed to take notice. It also seemed to have a variety of aliases—such as reverse instruction, reverse teaching, or backwards teaching—and could be done several ways. Regardless of when, where, or how, and no matter what name you assign it, it seemed that this flipped classroom was the approach that many teachers were using and that its benefits were outweighing the drawbacks.

It was at this same time that I realized that, as a second language (L2) instructor at a university, I both needed and wanted to consider this flipped model in my L2 classes. Why? First, I needed to because a main objective of my teaching is to prepare students to succeed in their coursework at the university. If it was becoming necessary for students to succeed in flipped classrooms, then I was going to have to prepare them for such settings and that would require that I flip my own classroom to some degree. Second, I wanted to adopt the flipped classroom model because I had been teaching for a long time and related to flipped adopters who said that they had been teaching the same course for many years and wanted to change things a bit. If my colleagues were feeling rejuvenated and their students were rejuvenated, why shouldn't I reap the same rewards and do the same for my students? Third, it simply sounded good. Interactive classes, a better relationship with students, more enjoyment in the classroom—these were all appealing.

Can the L2 Classroom Be Flipped?

But how does one flip a classroom and, more specifically, how does one flip the ESL classroom? Most of what I had read described the basic process as follows: (1) instructors videotape their lectures, (2) students watch the lectures outside of class, and (3) class time is spent on discussion or activities related to the lecture content. But this process concerned me for two reasons. First, I had textbooks I liked using and didn't want to give them up. Reading, writing, listening, and speaking strategies and instruction, vocabulary and grammar content, and other textbook material were sound and consisted of what I needed students to learn and practice in order to move beyond the ESL classroom. Second, I had a fear of technology, at least of making my own technology, and the thought of videotaping myself was simply too daunting to consider. I've never liked myself in photographs, so I couldn't imagine trying to put myself in videos. Besides, what was I going to record? I didn't formally lecture much in my ESL classrooms. I presented the material in the textbook, and the closest thing I had to traditional lectures were the audio passages on CD that accompanied a listening textbook or were posted on various websites. Was I supposed to record myself talking about the strategies that were already presented so well in the textbooks? That didn't seem to make much sense to me. That's when I started thinking of other ways to flip and to do what I started calling a "semi-flip."

Every discipline has unique features and needs that others don't; to me, ESL is no different. Our needs and our students' needs sometimes don't fit the mold of other classes and other methods. So maybe our flipped model is different, too. I mentioned to my editor that it might be worth exploring the idea of a simple instructor's manual, for lack of a better term, for ESL teachers with a few ideas and some sources. I thought it might include things that had worked for me—ideas that are simple enough to implement, ideas that won't create a lot of extra work for the already busy ESL instructor, and ideas that use existing content (online and in texts) to help teachers apprehensive about implementing technology and who like the material that already exists. Hence, this short resource was born.

These ideas led me to flip my ESL classes; some are more flipped than others, but all are more interactive. I primarily teach listening, speaking, and writing courses at the university, but the courses also contain components of reading, vocabulary, and grammar. It seemed easiest, to me, to flip listening since much of the audio and visual was already provided and/or could be found online, so that's what I did. It took a bit more thought for me to implement a flipped learning model with other skills, such as speaking or reading, but I have found some ideas that work well.

The way we learn and the way we teach has changed. In looking back at my own experiences in the classroom as a student, I wasn't in a flipped classroom. It very often was me taking notes during a lecture and then going home and studying those notes and doing whatever homework was assigned. There were times I never really interacted with my peers and certainly not with the instructor. Might I have been more motivated if class time had included discussion about the lecture or chapter content?

Other Labels for a Flipped Classroom

I decided to flip my classroom, but to do that in earnest, I wanted to know more about flipped learning as a concept. I discovered other terms—blended learning, mixed-mode learning, hybrid learning. Was one of these models better?

Blended learning is a combination of traditional classroom learning with online learning. It's <u>not</u> a distance education course or an online course because there is some face-to-face time. It replaces only some of the classroom time. Also sometimes referred to as **mixed-mode** learning or **hybrid** learning, it can be a reasonable alternative at institutions with student populations that cannot attend classes full-time since classroom time can be significantly less than what is considered traditional. This learning model does not reduce the amount of material that is covered, nor does it completely free students from the classroom; they are required to attend scheduled class meetings. With blended learning, a website of some sort is necessary as is the availability of and proficiency in technology for both the instructors and the learners. In many cases, course management systems serve the blended learning model well. Some people say flipped learning is a type of blended, mixed-mode, or hybrid learning with the blend of video, class time, and type of interaction in the classroom varying in each case. Although I was currently in a setting where technology availability and proficiency wasn't a problem for my students, I wasn't in a position to cut my face-to-face time in half, nor was I at a point where I was willing to sacrifice all of my textbooks, especially in cases where I had a textbook that was working well. I refocused my attention on flipped classrooms because I knew that my schedule would not change and that I would be required to have the same number of class meetings. I began to alter my thinking a little and started approaching this, not as a classroom model, but as a learning model. I started referring to what I was doing as **flipping the learning,** as opposed to teaching in a flipped classroom.

By focusing on the term **flipped learning,** I was able to dispel the myth that I had to record lectures for students to watch at home. According to the Flipped Learning Network website at <u>flippedlearning.org</u>, "Flipped learning occurs when direct instruction is moved from the group teaching space to the individual learning environment. Class time is then used for higher-order, active problem solving by students and one-to-one or small group interactions with the teacher." Shifting my own views helped me see that flipped learning allowed me to focus on moving the higher-order skills, such as analysis, synthesis, or evaluation, into the classroom and asking students to work on lower-order skills, such as knowledge and comprehension, at home. I moved what used to be group work and/or homework outside of class and moved what used to be homework projects (group or individual) inside the classroom. This change shifted the emphasis from method to learning. Despite the shift, I could still decide how I was going to present content and I didn't necessarily need to record lectures or videotape myself. Not having a flipped classroom in the traditional sense allowed me to keep all that worked well with my ESL classes—the materials, the methods, the face-to-face time—and better differentiate instruction and improve classroom dynamics to make my classroom just as important as the courses students took to earn a degree. This change allowed me even more time to interact with students outside of class during office hours or via email.

Flipped learning became my goal. Some of my flipping only required small changes to lesson plans and instruction. Other ideas were loftier, and I slowly started incorporating those into my ESL classroom and adapting them for ESL specifically. After all, I wanted my classroom to be effective. So far, I seem to be reaping some of the same rewards as instructors who had adopted the flipped model before me.

How To Use This Book

Throughout this book, I provide some simple ways to start flipping and places to find ideas for interactive activities, such as instructor's manuals, additional publisher's materials, or other online resources. Examples of textbook material are included where appropriate. These examples are provided to illustrate *how* materials can be used in a flipped setting and *how* the methodology can be applied to any materials you use. Many ideas that have worked for me are provided throughout Part 2 (Advantages) and Part 3 (Strategies). They can be adapted for use with levels (beginning, intermediate, advanced) and for skills other than those shown. Suppose the example illustrates content from an EAP reading class. For example, Figure 17 includes a reading strategy box on annotating. If annotating is part of your lesson plan, then the flipped lesson idea presented here could be applied directly to your course. However, this particular lesson could also be a guide for how to flip any reading strategy that is part of your lesson plan. This idea could also be adapted for other skills as well. The textbook samples provided range from textbooks used in a variety of settings, including adult education, IEP, and EAP courses. All samples can be adapted and serve only as a model of the way to flip.

The examples included come from textbooks I use or content I've developed. When copyright laws prevented me from showing specific textbook ideas, I found similar activities in University of Michigan Press resources, but the ideas can certainly and easily be applied and used with a variety of textbooks. Because of copyright laws and space limitations, the examples from textbooks are not reproducible. Bear in mind also that these sample activities appear in isolation and do not always contain <u>all</u> of the content needed to use them. As a result, the sample activities were not provided to be used as is but provided as examples of *how to* flip that particular kind of lesson or where to find additional ideas about how to flip a particular type of lesson. Additionally, although the activities were used with a flipped learning model, they can also be used regardless of the "blend" you choose: flipped or blended, hybrid, or mixed-mode. In some cases, the textbook examples are included to illustrate typical activities available and to show how they are used in traditional classrooms versus flipped or blended classrooms. Others are included to illustrate easy ways to make the in-class time more interactive. These ideas are presented to stimulate ideas and/or to prompt you to look more deeply at the supplemental material accompanying the textbooks or content you are currently using. Some details as to how to convert material in general into flipped lessons are also included. Specific ideas are provided in Part 3, but those same techniques can be applied to all examples provided throughout this book and to your textbooks of choice.

PART 1—An Overview

What Is Flipped Learning?

First, think about traditional learning. By most definitions, traditional learning involves instruction focused on the teacher. The instructor is the expert and shares his or her knowledge, most often through lectures, with the students. Flipped learning is different. Flipped learning occurs when students are exposed to the instruction outside of the classroom and when class time is used as a means to apply that newly found outside knowledge through activities. It also turns Bloom's taxonomy upside down. Rather than class time focusing on the lower level of Bloom's taxonomy (knowledge and comprehension), class time is spent on higher-level skills (application, analysis, synthesis, and evaluation), which are often not practiced much or developed well (see Figures 1 and 2).

Let's focus on what we first think of when we hear about flipped classrooms. In its simplest terms, **a flipped classroom** is one in which material traditionally presented or done in class is assigned as homework and tasks usually assigned as homework are now done in the classroom. One of flipped learning's most common forms involves technology: Students watch the instructors' lectures online at home and then participate in discussions, solve problem sets, work collaboratively on assignments, or develop projects (or something similarly group-oriented or interactive) in class. However, this isn't the only way to implement flipped learning. **Flipped learning doesn't have to involve videos or technology at all.** Instruction can be delivered via reading just as easily as it can be from videos.

Although it seems that iterations of the flipped model have existed over the years, many credit Jonathan Bergmann and Aaron Sams. In 2004, they were teaching chemistry at a Colorado high school. Students were missing class due to sporting events and activities and often struggled to keep up with the material. Sams found an article about software that would allow teachers to record PowerPoint slides and distribute them online. In 2007, Bergmann amd Sams tried it. They recorded their lessons using this soft-

Figure 1. Bloom's Taxonomy in a Traditional Learning Classroom

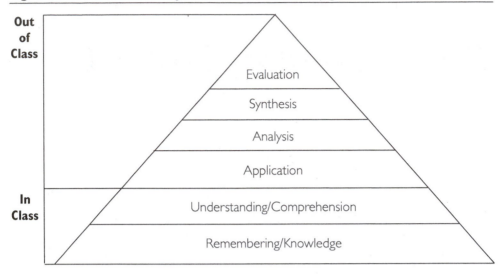

Figure 2. Bloom's Taxonomy in a Flipped Learning Classroom

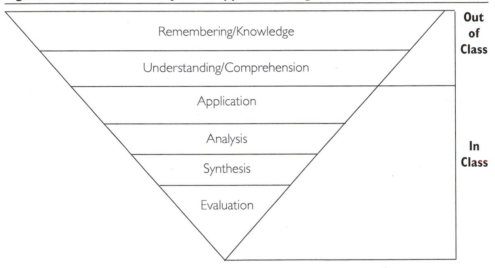

ware and posted the lectures online so that all students could access them. Since then, they no longer lecture in front of the classroom, and they often talk about the different role they now have in educating their students.

If instructors are no longer lecturing in class, how does this change the ESL classroom where instructors are preparing students for other college courses, for professions, or for basic survival in an English-speaking setting? What does it mean for instructors who use textbook material (or their own material) and teach that content in class? Any instructor now pursuing flipped learning requires students to study the topic on their own and uses classroom time to apply this newfound knowledge by completing exercises, solving practical problems, using authentic materials, working collaboratively on assignments, or participating in discussions and debates. In this new learning model, the instructor doesn't spend the entire class time lecturing; rather, she or he is almost, in a sense, tutoring or mentoring—helping students as needed rather than giving the instruction. Students still have homework (and maybe more than before), and the instructor is still a vital part of the learning experience.

It's important to note what flipped classrooms are not. They are not synonymous with online video instruction, and they are not structureless working environments. Even if an instructor uses video, students are not spending the bulk of their time at the computer working in isolation. It's actually quite the opposite. The most important thing, according to Bergmann, Overmyer, and Wilie (2013), is the interaction and meaningful activities that take place during class time—the time when the instructor is with the student in the classroom.

A flipped class is not an online course, is not a massive open online course (MOOC), and does not replace instructors. Rather, flipped learning makes the instructor even more valuable to the student because she or he is more accessible when students are working interactively and engaged in learning. Face-to-face time is likely to increase rather than decrease. Flipped classrooms are a way to increase interaction and personalized contact. An instructor who is flipping, especially in an ESL setting, is even more valuable because she or he is more than simply the person presenting text material. Since students are paying to learn, they tend to appreciate this increased face-to-face time and interaction with the teacher. Bergmann, Overmyer, and Wilie (2013) summarize flipped classrooms as being:

- a means to increase interaction and personalized **contact time** between students and teachers
- an environment where students take **responsibility for their own learning**
- a classroom where the teacher is not the "sage on the stage" but the **"guide on the side"**
- a **blending** of direct instruction with constructivist learning
- a classroom where students who are **absent** due to illness or extracurricular activities, such as athletics or field-trips, don't get left behind

- a class where content is permanently **archived** for review or remediation
- a class where all students are **engaged** in their learning
- a place where all students can get a **personalized** education (retrieved from www.thedailyriff.com/articles/the-flipped-class-conversation-689.php).

As far as my own teaching was concerned, it wasn't enough anymore for me to follow a textbook, assign practice activities and worksheets as homework, go over answers in class, and then give a test or some sort of evaluative assignment. Students were doing fine, but was I really preparing them for success, whether that be for college courses or simply for using English beyond immediate need in the ESL classroom? They certainly weren't engaging with the content as much as they could have, and if that wasn't happening, then how would they survive when faced with content in general education classes, coursework in their majors, or non-academic content such as that encountered in professional or life-skills settings where they really need to understand and **use** content? Flipping the classroom seemed to offer a way to address these issues. A discussion of many other benefits for instructors and students are detailed in the next section.

PART 2—Advantages

Benefits of Flipping

Students Have the Time They Need to Understand

At some point, it seems that all instructors face the same question when presenting content in class. Think about what happens after you've covered the material you planned for the class period. In **listening**, this might mean that you've presented a listening strategy and played the listening passage; in **writing**, it may mean you've presented an organizational format, grammar point, or something you're expecting the students to then practice or produce; in **reading**, you might have presented a reading strategy; or in **speaking**, you may have presented a list of common words or phrases appropriate for a certain situation. Then, you ask some version of this question: *Does everyone understand?* and are greeted with versions of Yes or No or, as happens to all instructors at some point, no response at all. It is at this time that instructors are faced with a decision. Do you move forward for those students who understand (or claim to)? Do you ask them to work on the exercises in the book? The risk, of course, is leaving behind the students who don't understand. Or, do you stop and answer questions, making sure the students who responded with some form of No understand before you move forward? Do you play the listening passage again, answer questions, or explain the same content again in different words? The risk here, of course, is losing the students who are ready to move forward to boredom or frustration. In either case, you lose time. If you play a listening passage again, you lose that many more minutes. The more advanced the students, the longer their listening passages, including in some cases entire lectures. Instructors can't always afford that much class time.

In the flipped model, time is less of an issue for students because they can take as much time as they need or want to go over the material. Students can work at their own pace and work for as long as they want or need in any way they want or need in order to comprehend the content. For listening tasks, they can stop the audio or rewatch the video. For written content, they can read and reread. They can stop to look up vocabulary words if desired. When students have tackled the content outside of class, they are all "on the same page" when they arrive in class and are much better prepared because they've spent their own definition of ample time with the content. Instructors know that they're all at the same starting point and can begin with the activities in the book or those that have been prepared. The students seem to be more comfortable with this as well. This structure lessens the peer pressure that some students feel to finish with the "faster" students, and it lessens the frustration that other students may feel when it takes the "slower" students longer to grasp content. Stress levels are also reduced because students are free to reread or listen again, and no one has to know if they listened once or three times or if they stopped reading to look up one vocabulary item or ten. It doesn't matter how many times students reread or relisten; in the end, they're practicing and that's giving them more time with English than when delivery of the material is confined to the classroom. While all instructors want to believe and hope that students go home and listen again on their own or practice more, we all know that this is not what happens.

Some activities from a reading textbook provide a simple example. The activities accompany a fairly long and challenging reading (a journal article) on stereotypes in the 5th edition of *Reader's Choice*. In a traditional class, students might read the article in class, perhaps taking turns reading paragraphs aloud. Maybe the instructor also stops after each paragraph and defines troublesome vocabulary. Or, perhaps students are given a certain amount of time to read silently. In the end, Exercises 1 and 2 in Figure 3 are completed in class.

But in this traditional scenario, sometimes students struggle. They are not able to read at their own pace and may not have had time to re-read. Other students may be fine. Depending on the level and range of capabilities, the instructor may never have time to complete the Critical Reading questions or the Discussion/Composition questions provided (see Figure 4), which are far more interactive and require students to not only comprehend, but analyze, evaluate, and synthesize.

In a flipped model, students read the passage at home and are able to take as much or as little time as they need. When they come to class, students will have already checked any unknown vocabulary and don't have to ask in front of their peers. Likewise, peers who already know those words aren't waiting while the instructor defines something they already know. The instructor may choose to assign Exercises 1 and 2 in Figure 3 as part of the homework. Then only a few minutes of class time are required to check answers, and the bulk of class time is spent on the activities that require critical thinking, application of the content, more interaction, and other higher-order skills.

Figure 3. Example of Activities Traditionally Completed after Reading

---

EXERCISE 1

The following questions check your understanding of the main ideas in "The Stereo-type of Stereotypes." Indicate if each of the statements below is true (T) or false (F) according to the article.

1. T / F   According to Yueh-Ting Lee, national stereotypes represent unjustified prejudices.
2. T / F   Some researchers believe that we need stereotypes to deal with a large and dangerous world.
3. T / F   Charles Stangor believes that stereotypes accurately reflect cultural or group differences.
4. T / F   Charles Stangor believes that stereotypes can be used by the powerful to harm the less powerful.
5. T / F   For much of the last century, psychologists and writers believed that stereotypes were invalid.
6. T / F   Our ancestors may have used stereotypes to survive in a complex and dangerous world.
7. T / F   Lee believes that understanding stereotypes can be helpful in understanding others.
8. T / F   Lee and Baron see no dangers in stereotypes.
9. T / F   The article demonstrates why further research is not necessary.

EXERCISE 2

Look back at the article to complete the following task. "The Stereotype of Stereo-types" presents a variety of points of view and research on stereotypes. Below is a list of researchers and writers cited in the article. Put a P next to the names of those who see positive effects of stereotypes. Put an N next to those who are reported to have negative opinions of stereotypes.

1. ____ Yueh-Ting Lee		4. ____ Gordon W. Allport	
2. ____ Charles Stangor		5. ____ Reuben M. Baron	
3. ____ Walter Lippman		6. ____ David C. Funder	

From: Silberstein, Clarke, & Dobson. (2008). *Reader's Choice, 5th Edition,* pages 118–119, University of Michigan Press.

Figure 4. Example of Activities Not Traditionally Completed after Reading

Critical Reading

1. What does the title "The Stereotype of Stereotypes" mean? Do you think that we have stereotypes about stereotypes?

2. In Paragraphs 6 and 7, the author contrasts the views of Stangor and Lee concerning the effects of stereotypes. With whom do you agree? When does a useful generalization about other people become a harmful stereotype?

3. Yueh-Ting Lee (Paragraph 11) believes that people can use stereotypes to help with conflict resolution. Can you give an example from your own experience? Do you agree or disagree with Lee?

4. a. Did you enjoy the joke that began this article? Why or why not? When they work, what makes such jokes funny? When are they not funny?

   b. The following question is meant in fun. Every culture has stereotypes and generalizations about other groups. If you or those in your home culture were writing the email message, what would be good and bad characteristics of different countries? Fill in the chart in the spirit of fun; be careful to respect the feelings of your classmates.

	Good	**Bad**
Food		
Car		
Art		
House		
Toilet Paper		

   c. Give examples of ways by which you might discover that your stereotypes are inaccurate.

Discussion/Composition

1. By and large, do you believe stereotypes are positive or negative? You will be debating this issue. In preparation, go through "The Stereotype of Stereotypes" and put a P next to any arguments that would support a positive view of stereotypes. Put an N next to negative arguments. Work with your classmates to develop a debate. (Do you believe that using a debate format to clarify your thoughts is a stereotypically North American way to proceed?)

2. If you were going to develop a high school curriculum on stereotypes, what would you teach? Work with your classmates to develop a list of ideas and a list of possible activities.

3. In Paragraph 5 the author says that many psychologists find Lee's opinions "about as welcome as a cut in their research grants." What does this mean? What does it tell us about scientists and their research grants? Can you make up other expressions using this phrasing, for example, "about as welcome as running out of gas in the desert"?

4. Below is a statement by Yueh-Ting Lee, quoted in the article (Paragraph 12).

   > Group differences, not prejudice, are the root cause of tension and conflict between various cultural and racial groups.

   What does this mean? Do you agree or disagree? Which do you think is the major cause of cultural conflict: real differences between groups or prejudice? Support your position orally or in writing by presenting reasons and examples.

From: Silberstein, Clarke, & Dobson. (2008). *Reader's Choice, 5th Edition,* pages 119–120, University of Michigan Press.

Instructors Have More Control of Class Time

In the end, this time-saving component extends beyond the students' time. It also creates more time for instructors, which is reflected in several ways. First, instructors can better monitor their class time. Using a flipped model means instructors do not have to allow a specific amount of time for the content delivery and do not have to factor in time for content questions or the playing or replaying of an audio component. Most instructors can relate to this issue: No matter how much time is allotted for questions about the content in the lesson plans, it always seems to be too little or too much. That factor lessens or disappears when a flipped model is incorporated. For example, in a more traditional model, instructors may allot time for a replaying of the listening passage. If the passage is 9 minutes long, you allow 18 minutes in your lesson plan. Yet instructors may still have to plan an activity to fill 9 minutes if it is a case in which students understand the passage adequately the first time and there is no need to play the audio again. There is always a risk of being "off" in the traditional model; either you have an extra activity that you don't get to use, or you planned to be further ahead because you assumed students didn't need the replay but then discovered that you would have to replay or review content.

In both scenarios, the instructor might be disappointed and some percentage of students is likely to be disappointed. In general, instructors face the concern that they didn't get far enough in the book or cover enough content because they used the time for a replay of audio or a review of content. Most instructors want to be able to cover all the content in the textbook, usually because students want to, but many times this is impossible. Students don't want to buy a textbook and then not be required to use all of it. Although instructors see the value in owning the textbook despite not covering every unit, students typically don't. Instructors can consistently cover more material in the textbooks when using the flipped model than when not. For example, many activities in the textbook can be used as flipping activities and/or easily converted into interactive activities rather than being skipped or used as "traditional" homework assignments.

For example, a synthesizing section from the *Four Point* series (*Reading and Writing Intro*), which is designed for intermediate EAP students, provides four possible activities that require higher-order thinking and offer the flexibility to be in-class, interactive activities (see Figure 5). In many cases, this last page of the unit may never be covered or perhaps only one activity would be used as a final evaluative project. However, if the other readings and practice activities are assigned as homework in a flipped classroom, more time exists for these projects to be used, and little or no extra preparation is required for the instructor. Also, think about the planning time. Consider a case where the listening or reading passage you are using is one that you have used before, which means that you don't have to listen or read it outside of class because you already know it.

In the flipped model, instructors and students both experience less frustration, less boredom, and less pressure. Figure 6 is an example from a listening textbook called *Academic Listening Strategies* and is labeled as "optional practice"; it is accompanied by a 26-minute video clip on lasers delivered by an electrical engineering professor. In a traditional classroom, watching the video takes at least half of a 50-minute class. If students understood the first time, students can complete the lower-order, comprehension questions during class. Depending on the population, it is likely that students would need to listen twice and therefore unlikely that an instructor will have time for students to complete, much less discuss, the important analysis questions about the lecture that could help them think about strategies that would be useful in other classes or settings (see Figure 6).

Figure 5. Examples of Higher-Order Skills and Interactive Activities

Synthesizing: Writing Projects

In-Class Assignments	Outside Assignments
Buck or Cather?	**You Should Read . . .**
Write a paragraph about similarities Buck and Cather shared and/or differences between them. In your paragraph, explain which writer you'd most like to read novels by and why. State which parts of the critical introductions helped you make your decision and cite as needed. **Suggested Length:** 300 words **Preparation:** none	Work with a group. Choose a novelist to research, write about, and present to the class. Include details about the novelist's life, works, and influences. Prepare a written report to submit. Create a presentation to give to the class about why this novelist is one worth reading. Include visuals in your presentation if you can (perhaps pictures of the author and of historical events from the time the novelist lived and/or wrote about). **Suggested Length:** 500 words **Preparation:** Light research in a library or online
My Prompt	**A Critical Introduction**
Imagine you are an instructor. Write a prompt that students should be able to answer using information from Reading 1 and/or Reading 2. Give the prompt to your teacher and get one that another student wrote. Now imagine that you are the student. Write a response to the prompt that one of your classmates wrote. Your instructor will tell you how much time you have to write. **Suggested Length:** 300 words **Preparation:** none	Choose your favorite novel, a novel you are reading now, or a novel you are familiar with. Do some light research online or in the library to determine the author's background, the themes, and the world events that may have influenced the author. Write a critical introduction for readers who are not familiar with the author or the events happening in the world at the time the novel was written. Self-edit and peer-edit before revising your writing to submit to your instructor. **Suggested Length:** 800 words **Preparation:** Light research in a library or online

From: Lockwood & Sippell. (2012). *Four Point Reading and Writing Intro*, page 233, University of Michigan Press.

Figure 6. Example of Listening Comprehension and Analysis Questions

TASK 8 (Optional practice)

You have already studied the first half of this lecture. For extra listening practice, listen to the second half, take notes, and answer the following comprehension questions. If you notice that you cannot answer of the following comprehension questions, you should find a method to compensate for what you missed. If, for example, you notice you couldn't answer Question 1, review your notes, listen to that part of the lecture again, and try to determine why you missed that information.

Comprehension Questions for Clip

1. What is "feedback" in a laser? What example does Professor Winful use to describe it?

    _____

    _____

    _____

2. What is "oscillation"? How does Professor Winful define it?

    _____

    _____

3. What is "pumping"?

    _____

    _____

    _____

4. How do mirrors affect the light in the laser cavity? How does this light come out of the cavity?

    _____

    _____

    _____

5. Why is laser light so directional?

    _____

    _____

    _____

6. What does it mean to "satisfy oscillation conditions"?

    _____

    _____

    _____

7. What does "out of phase" mean? What does "in phase" mean?

    _____

    _____

    _____

8. What are two major applications for laser technology that Professor Winful talks about?

    _____

    _____

    _____

Analysis Questions

TASK 9

1. What strategy did you use when confronted with the many drawings on the board? Did you copy only the drawings in your notes, or did you include some of the commentary?

    _____

    _____

    _____

2. If you had a strong background in physics or electrical engineering, this was probably an easy lecture for you. You can see the importance of background when approaching a lecture and the effect background has on your comprehension. If you did not have a strong background in these subjects and missed some concepts, what strategies did you use to compensate?

    _____

    _____

    _____

3. You may have also noticed in this lecture how Professor Winful builds on each concept he presents. If you missed the definition of coherency, for example, early in the lecture, you might have trouble later in the lecture. In addition, you may become fatigued toward the end of a lecture. In addition, you may become fatigued toward the end of a lecture. These factors may cause a kind of compounding of comprehension difficulties toward the latter half of any lecture. What strategies could you use to be sure your comprehension at the end of the lecture is solid?

    _____

    _____

    _____

From: Salehzadeh. (2005). *Academic Listening Strategies,* pages 87–89, University of Michigan Press.

Improved Caliber of Work

Related to, or perhaps as a result of, the time benefits from flipping is the better work from students. When students grasp the content—whether strategies, ESL content, or the content in a reading or listening passage—they perform better on activities in the book; participate more readily, more quickly, and with greater quantity and quality in class discussions; and/or produce better work on their own.

For example, imagine a reading strategy, and then think about a reading in a textbook—maybe it's about a president, maybe it's about an artist, or maybe it's about steroid use in sports. In a more traditional classroom model, students learn the strategy and then apply it to the reading. Then comprehension questions can then be answered in class or assigned as homework, and there may be discussion questions. However, many students won't be able to perform well or answer questions quickly about content that is new to them, and it may happen that time elapses before the discussion questions can even be addressed. If the flipped approach is taken, students can do the reading as homework and can apply the strategy that ideally prepares them to better understand the content, and they can read, reread, look up vocabulary, and better comprehend the actual content. When they come to class, students are better prepared, which leads to more insightful discussions about what they read. They can better participate in a discussion about the president, the artist, or steroid use in sports. This ability to discuss and use content is what they're going to have to do in future classes and in other settings (academic and professional).

A flipped model also offers some flexibility. In a classroom where the planned reading is assigned as homework, instructors can ask students to read in class, ensuring that the strategy is being practiced and that students are reading the passage in depth. This format also then allows students to use the actual reading content.

To give an example of how the flipped model can work, whether students are reading in or out of the classroom, think of questions that students often read; for example, a question that begins something like this: *In Paragraph 3, the writer* . . . . If the flipped model has been adopted to some degree, the students don't have to go back and reread Paragraph 3 word for word before answering. Additionally, some students aren't waiting while other students do reread the paragraph to be discussed. Everyone has already read and comprehended the content outside of class. As a result, discussions and answers are more thorough.

Look at Question 4 in Figure 7, which accompanies a reading about alternative energy in the textbook titled *Choice and Consequence*. In a traditional classroom in which the reading has been done in class silently or aloud, students likely need time to reread Paragraph 7, and many will need time to digest the contents before being able to tackle Question 4 about inferences. In some cases, students may even need to reread the paragraphs before Paragraph 7. These occurrences stifle interactivity, lead to silence, and make the classroom less dynamic. In a flipped model where students come to class already having read the reading as often or as deeply as necessary to solidify their own individual understanding, Question 4 can be addressed more quickly within the group setting. Additionally, the Reading Critically box shown in Figure 7 would most likely be assigned as homework, so students would already be familiar with inferences and be able to answer the question. In the traditional model, the inference box would likely have been presented after the reading, which would not give students time to fully grasp the concept before having to try to produce an inference in the next activity.

Additionally, when they see opinion questions like, *What do you think should happen to baseball players who use steroids?* they can answer quickly. Not only do students seem to better enjoy class settings full of interaction, but they also are able to apply content, are able to use higher-order and critical-thinking skills, and are better prepared for life beyond the ESL classroom.

Figure 7. Example of Questions that Follow a Reading Passage

Reading Critically: Inferences

Making inferences means drawing conclusions or recognizing an author's opinions when they are not directly stated. Authors often imply or suggest ideas with careful choice of words. In these cases, the reader has to "read between the lines" to fully understand the reading.

When making an inference, the reader makes an educated guess based on the information that is written. Be careful not to confuse inferences with information that is stated in the article. Facts, and even opinions, are often **directly stated by the author**. Inferences are assumptions or conclusions made by the reader based on what the writer has implied.

Answer the questions about the reading. Then discuss your answers with your classmates.

1. Who is the intended audience for this article? How do you know?

   _____

2. What is the implied main point or thesis of this article?

   _____

3. Does the author show bias for or against genetically modified foods? How do you know? <u>Hint</u>: Look for clues in the introduction and conclusion.

   _____

4. What can be inferred from Paragraph 7 about moving GMF from the laboratory to the marketplace?

   _____

From: Tunceren & Benson. (2010). *Choice and Consequence* (2010), page 131, University of Michigan Press.

This same improved caliber of work can be seen regardless of the skill or content being taught. In a writing classroom, students are often taught the material or concept and then are sent home to produce a piece of writing on their own. In a flipped model, students can read the concept on their own and then produce their writing in class. This structure is likely to produce better writing since students have their peers and the instructor there to offer input and feedback during the writing process. Revisions are applied before the submission of the assignment, making it a stronger draft than what originally would be submitted during the next class period and reducing the opportunity for plagiarism.

For example, the content in Figure 8 from *Academic Writing for Graduate Students, 3rd Edition,* can be easily adapted from a traditional to a flipped classroom. In a traditional classroom, the instructor will probably present the information in the figure on the moves in a research paper introduction, and then students will complete Task Two. At some point, students will be given a homework assignment requiring them to write an introduction. Applying this on their own may prove challenging, but in a flipped model, students would read the information about creating a research space and perhaps even complete Task Two as homework. Writing the introduction would be done in class as a writing workshop. Peers would be able to consult with each other and the instructor would be available and on hand to answer questions.

Figure 8. Example of Writing Content and Practice

Creating a Research Space

As you may have discovered, the introductions of research papers typically follow the pattern in Figure 16 in response to two kinds of competition: competition for readers and competition for research space. This rhetorical pattern has become known as the create-a-research-space (or CARS) model (Swales, 1990).

FIGURE 16. Moves in Research Paper Introductions

Move 1—Establishing a research territory

    a. by showing that the general research area is important, central, interesting, problematic, or relevant in some way (optional)

    b. by introducing and reviewing items of previous research in the area (obligatory)[*]

Move 2—Establishing a niche[**]

    by indicating a gap in the previous research or by extending previous knowledge in some way (obligatory)

Move 3—Occupying the niche

    a. by outlining purposes or stating the nature of the present research (obligatory)

    b. by listing research questions or hypotheses (PISF[***])

    c. by announcing principal findings (PISF)

    d. by stating the value of the present research (PISF)

    e. by indicating the structure of the RP (PISF)

---

[*] The one exception to this occurs in certain RPs that deal with "real world" problems, as in Engineering. In some cases, Move 1 deals with these problems without a literature review and the previous research on attempted solutions is postponed to Move 2 (see the text on pages 335–336).

[**] In ecology, a niche is a particular microenvironment where a particular organism can thrive. In our case, a niche is a context where a specific piece of research makes particularly good sense.

[***] PISF = probable in some fields, but rare in others.

TASK TWO

We begin our more careful analysis with an introduction to a research paper from the humanities. The paper has been adapted from one John Swales wrote for a History of Art seminar he audited on nineteenth-century realism. Read it and answer the questions.

Thomas Eakins and the "Marsh" Pictures

❶ Thomas Eakins (1844–1916) is now recognized as one of the greatest American painters, alongside Winslow Homer, Edward Hopper, and Jackson Pollock. ❷ Over the last thirty years, there have been many studies of his life and work,[1] and in 2002 there was a major exhibition devoted entirely to his art in his home city of Philadelphia. ❸ His best-known pictures include a number of rowing and sailing scenes, several domestic interiors, the two large canvasses showing the surgeons Gross and Agnew at work in the operating theater, and a long series of portraits, including several of his wife, Susan McDowell. ❹ The non-portraits are distinguished by compositional brilliance and attention to detail, while the portraits—most of which come from his later period—are thought to show deep insight into character or "psychological realism."[2] ❺ In many ways, Eakins was a modern late nineteenth century figure since he was interested in science, in anatomy, and in the fast-growing "manly sports" of rowing and boxing. ❻ In his best work, he painted what he knew and whom he knew, rather than being an artist-outsider to the scene in front of him. ❼ Among Eakins' pictures, there is a small series of scenes painted between 1873 and 1876 showing hunters preparing to shoot at the secretive marsh birds in the coastal marshes near Philadelphia. ❽ Apart from a chapter in Foster (1997), this series has been little discussed by critics or art historians. ❾ For example, these pictures were ignored by Johns in her pioneering 1983 monograph,[3] perhaps because

---

[1] Book-length studies include Hendricks (1974), Johns (1983), Fried (1987), Wilmerding (1993), Foster (1997), and Berger (2000).

[2] The question of what actually makes a work of art "realistic" is, of course, one of the most discussed issues in the history of art, and will not be directly addressed in this paper. For analyses of realism, see, among others, Nochlin (1990).

[3] Johns' book is an example of the "new" art history with its detailed attention to the *social* conditions and circumstances that give rise to a particular form of art.

their overall *smallness* (physically, socially and psychologically) did not fit well with her book's title, *Thomas Eakins: The Heroism of Modern Life.* ❿ These pictures are usually thought to have come about simply because Thomas Eakins used to accompany his father on these hunting/shooting trips to the marshes.[4] ⓫ However, in this paper I will argue that Eakins focused his attention on these featureless landscapes for a much more complex set of motives. ⓬ These included his wish to get inside the marsh landscape, to stress the hand-eye coordination between the shooter and "the pusher," and to capture the moment of concentration *before* any action takes place.

1. Divide the text into the three basic moves.

2. How many paragraphs would you divide the text into? And where would you put the paragraph boundaries?

3. Look at Figure 16 again. Where in this Introduction would you divide Move 1 into 1a and 1b?

4. What kind of Move 2 did you find?

5. What kind of Move 3a did you find?

6. Underline or highlight any words or expressions in Sentences 1 through 4 that have been used "to establish a research territory."

7. How many citations are there in the text and footnotes?

8. Footnotes and endnotes are widely used in the humanities. Consider carefully the four footnotes in this Introduction. Do you think that this information is rightly footnoted, or do you think sometimes it would have been better in the main text? Conversely, is there material in the main text that you would have put in footnotes? What do your decisions tell you about the use of notes?

---

[4] Eakins contracted a bad case of malaria on one of these trips, and this brought his visits—and this series of paintings—to an end.

From: Swales & Feak. (2012). *Academic Writing for Graduate Students, 3rd Edition*, pages 331–333, University of Michigan Press.

Applying Skills to College Courses and Real Life

There seems to be a point for many students where they need to be able to apply what they are reading. College life beyond the ESL classroom does not replicate what students see in textbooks. Take college reading, for example. At some point, students are no longer expected to read a passage and then answer a few multiple choice questions about it. They need to read, fully comprehend, and then apply the content to essay questions, use it in research papers, reference it in discussions, or synthesize it with other material. The same rings true for listening. Students need to be able to listen to lectures and not just answer a few questions about the content. They need to be able to connect the lecture content to textbook material, discuss it with classmates, or use it for a group project. Students will also need to use certain academic speaking phrases and apply them in seminars, conversations, and group discussions with native speakers. In a work setting, they will not be required to have to read a business report for their boss and then answer a few multiple choice questions about it. They're going to have to summarize the report and apply information from it to their job.

Better Grades

Can the flipped model raise grades? New studies are being conducted, but in general, the consensus is Yes. *The Atlantic* published an article, "The Post-Lecture Classroom: How Will Students Fare?" by Robinson Meyer (2013). In it, the author details a three-year study of a foundational PhD course at the University of North Carolina. The first year was taught using a traditional format, and the following two years were taught using a flipped model. On the same examination, students improved 2.5 percent and 2.6 percent respectively. Overall, student performance on the same final exam improved by 5.1 percent (Meyer, 2013). Comments from students indicated that they preferred the flipped model.

Although debate about the flipped model's influence on test scores and performances exists, there are some statistics coming to light and more studies being conducted. However, it isn't solely those numbers that influenced me so much as simply the improved attitudes and general mood of the classroom, which cannot easily be measured quantitatively, other than asking students what they like about the class and its structure. However, a study published by Classroom Window (2012) included a survey of approximately 500 teachers, and responses indicated that 66 percent of students improved their standardized test scores, but also that 80 percent of teachers had students whose attitudes about learning improved. This data is appealing to many instructors who not only want their students to succeed, but who also want their students to enjoy learning. Avoiding boredom, which a flipped model can help accomplish, might be one factor that contributes to improved student attitudes.

Reduced Tedium and Increased Interaction

We all know that you can't please all the people all the time, yet sometimes it feels as if we instructors are expected to please all the students all the time. Flipped learning can help. The boredom factor might decrease when some flipping is incorporated. Why? Perhaps, in some part, this boredom factor is again partially tied to the time factor. Instructors are not forced to decide when to continue class and when to replay or re-explain concepts. But, besides this, the flipped classroom is far more interactive. The "boring" parts are done at home. Students also seem to do better with the content when they can read in the quiet of their home or at the library rather than when trying to keep up with others, and they don't seem to "hate" the material as much.

Are students even aware that a classroom is being flipped? If instructors don't tell them, then won't they do whatever is assigned? To some degree, don't students expect some homework? Students also begin to realize on their own that this new type of homework takes far less time than the "traditional" homework, which helps gain buy-in from students in terms of doing the reading or listening (or whatever assignment) at home. Instructors need to ensure that the in-class work is as interactive and as useful as possible so that students want to participate. Plus, listening to an online lecture is appealing to the current generation of students. Today's students grew up playing video games and using computers, and they seem to like them. They are not afraid of the technology and use it hours and hours every day. Listening to an online lecture is almost welcome. In fact, sometimes it seems they don't consider this homework, or if they do, they don't mind doing it as much. Students from the video game generation don't mind listening to a CD or watching a DVD or online lecture at home because they have lived with technology all their lives. They don't know how to live without these kinds of technologies, unlike previous generations of students. At the 2013 Teaching Professor Technology Conference, several presenters addressed the fact that teaching has to change because fewer students today are read-write learners.

In general with ESL, it seems that not only is some of this "homework" less time-consuming than traditional homework, but it's also easier for students to do on their own. They don't always need help with knowledge and comprehension; they do usually need help with the higher-level skills. Flipping also seems to make coming to class less of a chore. Classes are filled with discussion, projects, and group work. It is more active; it's no longer about sitting still and listening to one person talk.

Group work and projects are used more in a flipped classroom. In a traditional model, students meet their groups and complete their projects outside of class. The pressure to create a good project is often overwhelming. In a flipped model, the project is developed in class with the instructor available if needed. All of this lessens pressure on students.

In a Reading Class

Even if an instructor only requires students to read the reading passage as homework and has them work on the subsequent comprehension activities in class, they can be done collaboratively with partners or in small groups. Students learn from other students sometimes just as well as they learn from an instructor. Members of the video-game generation learn by doing and seem to think better when interacting with others. They are also more resourceful when working together. Students can check or compare answers in class. Discussion questions are now literally *discussion* questions. When this happens, it creates opportunities for students to work in groups and then present their answers to the other groups. Students do seem to respond well to this, and class is perceived as more "fun" or "useful," even though instructors know that the traditional approach is "useful" as well.

In a Writing Class

Consider a writing class. In writing, an instructor presents the material in the textbook, perhaps a strategy box on connectors followed by a practice activity. Then, the instructor assigns the homework, which might be a paragraph or essay using connectors (or whatever strategy was just discussed in class). In the flipped model, though, students read the strategy box and do the practice activity at home, and then in class, students review their answers with the teacher and complete the writing assignment.

I sometimes ask my students how long it took them to complete the homework assignments. It may have taken hours, far longer than probably necessary. They tell me it's because they're trying to make it perfect, referring back to the textbook, looking for samples, or still trying to understand the textbook content in general. In a flipped model, when I ask students to read the textbook content and complete practice activities at home, they reported that it took far less time than the writing assignment itself.

I have found that students seem to like comparing answers, discussing differences, and finishing their writing when they can collaborate with each other or consult with me in the classroom. Class isn't as tedious because they're actually doing something and are engaged rather than following along in a book. They feel they are doing their "homework" in class rather than having to do it outside. They don't view reading a few pages outside the class as "hard" or "time-consuming" homework, and some don't consider it homework at all. The traditional writing workshop style of class doesn't fit the more well-known flipped classroom definition because no material was videotaped, but it fits the basic model in that their homework has now become the classwork.

In Other Classes

Other skills, such as listening, speaking, or reading, can be even more dynamic with discussions, activities, and/or projects. Instructor's manuals are rich sources of Expansion Activities. Before I began to flip, I read all the good ideas in my instructor's manuals and wished I could find time to do all of them. I am finally getting the chance to implement some of them.

For example, the multi-skills textbook *What Makes America Tick?* is accompanied by an online instructor's guide. In Unit 2, which discusses the U.S. between world wars, there is a list of popular songs in a small section called Music Box, a section called At the Movies listing *The Grapes of Wrath* and *Of Mice and Men,* a reading about the New York Stock Exchange, and information about the beginning of the national park program. In a traditional classroom, most instructors are hard-pressed to make their way through all of the readings, questions, and assorted activities in the book, so these extra sections and readings are not used. But in a flipped model, more of these readings and activities can be done at home, which allows for interaction and application in the classroom and some other "fun" activities from the instructor's manual. Instructor's guides save instructors a lot of work by providing ideas suited to a flipped classroom (see Figure 9).

Figure 9. Example of Ideas Provided in Instructor's Manuals

Expansion Activities for Unit 1

1. Take one of the songs from the Music Box section and create a cloze exercise from the lyrics that leaves out every 7th word (the number of words or their pattern can be changed to meet the needs and skills of the students). Cloze exercises will help in vocabulary expansion but are also good practice for pronunciation and listening. Extend this activity by asking students if they liked the lyrics or the music. Also ask them how the lyrics are important to the times.

2. Bring copies of the stock reports from a newspaper or show them online. Let students see how some are up and some are down. Ask students to create their own stock market portfolio of five stocks they'd like to invest in and explain their choices. If time allows, give them time to do the research outside of class for a more thorough analysis or let them follow the stock prices for an extended period of time and then present the results.

3. Watch Ken Burns' series *The National Parks: America's Best Idea* (check local PBS listings). Clips are available at www.pbs.org/national_parks/. Ask students to choose one national park to research and create a brochure about it for their classmates.

4. Assign an excerpt from *The Grapes of Wrath* or *Of Mice and Men* to each student. Ask students to explain their excerpt to two other students. Encourage the speaker to be descriptive (review Unit 1) and the listeners to employ backchanneling strategies.

From: Instructor's Manual to accompany *What Makes America Tick? 2nd Edition.* (2012). University of Michigan Press.

What makes students buy into the concept of a flipped ESL classroom? Is there one answer or is it a combination of things? If we consider the benefits thus far, they are all motivating factors: the time being saved, the reduced peer pressure and reduced stress to understand quickly, the more interactive nature of the classroom, and the idea that they're "doing their homework in class." The flipped model often results in each class meeting being different. Rather than a lecture, reading, or strategy each time, students participate in different activities. Class seems less tedious to them. As previously mentioned, even though they are doing homework, sometimes they don't see it as such. In the writing class described on page 25, students perceived the writing assignment as homework. They likely feel instructors are not assigning homework at all by having them write in class. Again, asking them to spend 15 minutes reading the writing strategy and completing a practice activity takes far less time than writing the actual essay. They're motivated to come to class because they know they're going to get their "homework" done and because they will have more access to the teacher.

Instructors in a Consultative Role

Common phrases being used in discussions of the flipped classroom model include "sage on the stage" and "guide on the side." The **sage on the stage** is the instructor who is the expert and delivers the content in a formal, lecture-style format. Students listen, take notes, and then go home and study. Students from many different parts of the world are very accustomed to this model. They believe the teacher is the expert and that they are to simply accept the information, memorize it, and then regurgitate it. They're also often comfortable with this model. However, in the United States, lectures and classes are more interactive than in other countries, and now the flipped model is becoming more popular in U.S. higher education institutions.

Today's students need to be prepared because the flipped model doesn't have a sage on the stage; instead, the instructor is a **guide on the side**. The students gain the knowledge or content outside the class and then apply what they learned. The guide on the side moves about the room, helping as needed, talking with groups, offering feedback on projects, and answering questions as they arise. Consider a vocabulary class. In a flipped model, an instructor might ask the students to learn the 20 words outside of class rather than presenting them in class. An instructor might even ask students to complete the fill-in-the-blank activity with the "best" vocabulary item (or whatever the activity is in the textbook) as homework. Whatever had been done in class would now be done outside of class. In class, the instructor could put students in small groups to check their answers to the activity and circulate and answer questions as needed. If one group had a question about why *affect* is better than *effect,* for example, the instructor could answer in greater detail for that group. Instructors don't have to hold everyone back while they answer a question that everyone does not have.

The guide-on-the-side approach also allows for more individual attention. This seems to be true especially in writing classes when students are working on their assignment or whatever used to be homework. They may not all be writing about the same topic, so the instructor is able to serve as a consultant to individuals in class as needed. Students tend to struggle to write or apply what was covered in class to their writing assignments. Even if they say they understand the assignment when they are in class, it's very hard for them to produce their own writing outside of class. What seems to happen is students go home, struggle to apply what was covered in class, and then sign up for an office hour or send an email message to the teacher. By incorporating a flipped model and asking students to read the textbook or learn the general concepts at home and do the writing in class, instructors are available to help students as they write their assignments, which in turn builds a consultative relationship between the instructor and student. In this model, students submit better writing, which can lead to better grades because the quality is better. Instructors build rapport and can differentiate instruction for students. Students seem to appreciate this consultative type of relationship and perhaps the instructor also is more accessible and is more well-liked than the sage on the stage.

Figure 10, from the first level of the *Vocabulary Mastery* series, provides an example of a vocabulary activity that can build rapport and differentiate instruction. (Differentiated instruction is the concept that different students are provided with different ways to learn the content. For example, they may receive other types of instructions or other materials to suit their readiness level, interests, and learning preferences. Being able to consider varieties of learning needs through options for instruction helps all students learn the material.) In a more traditional setting, this exercise is skipped altogether or, if used, elicits questions about what is right and what is wrong, and those questions are often different for each student. In a flipped setting, the words have already been studied at home and students can be put into groups to make the word associations. The instructor can move from group to group to address questions.

Figure 10. Example of Vocabulary Activity that Can Build Rapport and Differentiate Instruction

---

Exercise 3: Word Associations

Which topic is each of these words associated with? Write each word under the appropriate topic. Some words may be used more than once. Add one more word to each list.

chemical	**generate**	**physical**
communications	**global**	**regulate**
consume	**labor**	**resources**
data	**military**	**survive**
equipment	**nuclear**	**sustainable**

Conflict	*Energy*	*Technology*
_____	_____	_____
_____	_____	_____
_____	_____	_____
_____	_____	_____
_____	_____	_____
_____	_____	_____
_____	_____	_____
_____	_____	_____

From: Wells. (2007). *Vocabulary Mastery 1*, page 101, University of Michigan Press.

May Reduce Absenteeism

One problem I have faced throughout my teaching career has been absenteeism. When I taught adult education, students were not required to be there. The program for which I taught was funded based on contact hours I had with students. Therefore, there was a financial reason to have as many students as possible. Absent students didn't translate into funding for books, salaries, or program needs. The program wanted and needed to have students, yet they weren't required to be there and I "competed" with students' jobs, families, and interest levels. Had I been using a flipped model then, I wonder whether interest levels might have been higher.

In my current university setting, I face this same "competition" from students' other disciplines. Although some of my students are required to enroll in English classes, many are not. Regardless of the requirements, my English class just never seems to be as important as classes in their fields of study. Absences often result from students needing to work on a project or paper for a class in their field, being up all night studying for an exam for another class, and/or attending a group meeting for a project when ESL class time was the only time that worked. It's hard to combat those types of excuses.

In a non-flipped ESL classroom, it isn't hard to skip English class. Students rationalize that they don't miss as much because they know the class covered page X to page Y and they know they can just copy the answers to the activity from a classmate the next day in class. In a flipped classroom, they will miss something if they skip. Even if they don't miss new content, they've missed something valuable because they are applying the content, are interactively engaged, are working on a group project, and/or are doing an activity that used to be homework. Most of this work cannot be made up easily, and the material that "used to be homework" and was finished in class is now additional homework for whoever missed class. Peer pressure can actually be an ally here. I don't, of course, promote the concept of peer pressure, but students tend to compete with or pressure each other without my prompting, and most of it is done in the spirit of healthy competitiveness. Students who are absent don't pull their fair share and can put a group behind schedule. Also, depending on the culture, students don't like to lose face by not showing up, not doing the work, or not participating as much as their classmates. They seem to have a harder time letting their classmates down than they do letting me, their instructor, down. A more interactive class is a more enjoyable class so students are more likely to *want* to attend.

Figure 11 is from a speaking skills book called *Taking Sides*, 2nd edition. For this particular activity, some of the objectives ask students to analyze a business problem and make recommendations for a course of action, learn to write a business memo, make difficult but common-sense personnel decisions, practice negotiating language and skills, and practice presentation skills. A negotiation game is included near the end of the unit after students are familiar with the case, the data, and the roles for the game. For the game, each student in the group is assigned a role and given a very clear objective. The group is given 20 minutes to make a decision. If a student doesn't come to class, she or he is likely to disappoint his or her peers, lose face, and miss out on an interactive (and often entertaining) activity that provides practice with some useful language. Additionally, if it is high stakes, their grade suffers.

Figure 11. Example of a Speaking Activity

Negotiation Game

[Exercise not shown in full.]

Objectives

Banks—to obtain the greatest amount of compensation and to convince DR to punish Adams for his theft

Adams—to pay the least amount of compensation

DR—to **mediate** the dispute in a way that makes everybody happy and that will appear to Sonny Berger to be wise and good for business

Procedure

The class will be divided into groups of three, with each student in every group being assigned one of three roles—Adams, Banks, or DR. Based on the case and your analysis of the "Relevant Data from Banks's Books," each player will argue his or her case. You will have a predetermined amount of time (around 20 min.) in which a decision must be made by DR.

From King. (2008). *Taking Sides, 2nd Edition,* page 127, University of Michigan Press.

Increased Use of Materials that Students Perceive as Important or Useful

One reason students might not always be motivated in the ESL classroom or choose to "skip" ESL class is because they aren't applying the content to anything they like or care about, to material they are interested in, or to other classes. Also, they aren't using the skills they just learned for anything other than ESL content or academic content; in other words, many students value skills they can use beyond academia, either in a professional setting or a life-skills setting. Flipping the classroom to some degree allows for more use of realia and/or application of the content, which then prepares students for their other classes or their future careers.

The flipped model allows instructors to let students bring in some of their own material to use or find relevant material of interest to them or their future major or career. To use a reading course as an illustration, an instructor can ask students to read the reading strategy box in the ESL text-book—say annotating is the skill—and to practice using the reading passage in the book. This reading might be done in class or the instructor may decide to let the students annotate in class. Regardless, there is class time for the instructor to put students in groups to discuss the strategy and share their annotations. Students can discuss what worked, what didn't work, or any variations they made to the skill. Instructors may also ask them to bring a textbook from another class or an article they're interested in reading (or required to read). Students can bring anything they want to read; what's important is that they're able to apply the strategy from the ESL textbook to outside material; the ESL content is then transferable. What's important to students is that they're accomplishing something for another class (the proverbial "kill two birds with one stone") or are applying it to something they are really interested in reading.

Figure 12 shows a sample of a writing strategy, summarizing, from the *Four Point* series. Also shown are the accompanying Expansion Activities from the Instructor's Manual that allow students to practice with material for another class, demonstrating for students the transferability of the skill (see Figure 13).

Figure 12. Example of a Writing Strategy that Can Be Flipped

Writing Strategy: Summary Writing

A summary is a piece of writing that summarizes another source. It has some similarities to paraphrasing:

- It keeps the original meaning.
- It requires using different words (use the same strategies as paraphrasing).
- It avoids plagiarism.
- It cites the original source.

A summary has some differences, too.

- It explains only the main ideas and most important supporting ideas.
- It does not include details.
- It is usually significantly shorter than the original.

Summaries are useful when writing a research paper. Writers can't include every detail from each source, but a summary gives the readers an idea of the research that the writers did. Because summaries are cited, readers can find the original sources if they want more details.

From: Lockwood & Sippell. (2012). *Four Point Reading and Writing Intro*, page 33, University of Michigan Press.

Figure 13. Example of Content in an Instructor's Manual Ideal for Flipping

Expansion Activity

The summarizing activity offers the opportunity to revisit spoken language as well as written language. Some phrases are suggested, but if students are using *Four Point Listening and Speaking Intro*, it's a good time to review language that encourages getting more information (see pages 3–4 in *Four Point Listening and Speaking Intro*). It's also a chance to introduce students to corpora and how they can be beneficial when speaking and writing in English. Use MICASE (Michigan Corpus of Academic Spoken English) as an example. MICASE is free and available to the public at www.elicorpora.info/. See the appendix in *Four Point Listening and Speaking 1* for ideas on using the corpus. Also introduce MICUSP (Michigan Corpus of Upper-Level Student Papers) for a written English corpus, which is available at www.elicorpora.info/. Challenge students to browse to look for other words and phrases used to discuss main ideas or purposes. Ask each student to bring one to class. Or, consider letting them search the written English corpus to find ways they can use this language in academic writing. Collect the phrases they find or have everyone write theirs on the board so students can compile a list to use in the future.

Expansion Activity

Consider having students bring a textbook from another class and encourage them to practice on material important to them. Or, for a more controlled practice on which to offer feedback, find an article that can be photocopied without infringing copyright. Distribute it to the class and ask students to annotate and/or summarize it. The summary could be collected for a grade. Find an appropriate rubric for the class at iRubric.com www.rcampus.com/indexrubric.cfm). The free website has rubrics already created for summaries (and other types of assignments) that can be borrowed, or it is easy to adapt one or create a new one.

From: Instructor's Manual to accompany *Four Point Reading and Writing Intro*. (2012). University of Michigan Press.

Figure 14 provides an example of an activity that practices a skill—retelling—that students often need beyond academia, that offers general knowledge about U.S. culture (the court system), and that provides very specific practice if the class includes future or current political science and law students.

Figure 14. Example of a Speaking Skill Needed Beyond the Classroom

JFK Memorial Hospital versus Heston

Objectives

- to learn the facts of a case for retelling, as is done in law schools

- to understand how a state supreme court decides a complicated case on paternalism and individual rights

Introduction

The following case was decided by the New Jersey Supreme Court. It is very relevant to the issue of "the right to die," which is much in the news. The case also deals with the very difficult issue of what to do when the right to practice one's own religion without government interference runs up against the right to life.

Procedure

As you read and reflect, keep in mind John Stuart Mill's thesis and the arguments for paternalism. Collaborate in retelling the story, making sure that no important details have been omitted. Discuss the issue in small groups, with each person giving his or her viewpoint. Finally, your teacher will tell you what the state supreme court decided.

From: King. (2008). *Taking Sides, 2nd Edition,* page 67, University of Michigan Press.

Overcoming Challenges When Flipping

There are some drawbacks, of course, to a flipped model. First, it may take time to earn student buy-in, especially if you decide to explain what you're doing to the students. That may not be an issue at all if students enjoy the interactive nature of the class and/or will lose face by not doing the work. They usually do buy in when they experience a game, debate, or something "fun" and realize what they'll miss if they don't do the homework. They may also buy in when they realize the time they're saving outside of class, either because the homework is done in class and/or they don't have to meet the instructor or peers outside of class. Also, students may accept the model when they realize how helpful English class can be now and how the skills they are practicing—whether reading, writing, listening, speaking, grammar-related, or vocabulary-related—will help them in their future academic studies or professional careers.

Second, it may take time to develop new activities to use in class. Many of us were accustomed to filling our class time by relying on the textbook material. Providing content might seem intimidating, but it's not, especially if you have a good textbook; the textbook is now the "homework." Instructor's manuals offer a wealth of activities that are easy to implement. Additionally, there are now many websites with available content, such as Academic Earth, or even ESL-specific lessons ready for use without having to record any material. Some simple online searches for "classroom ideas for X topic" can generate a lot of ideas. For example, if an instructor is teaching a listening class and decides the best way to practice a skill is to listen to a lecture on air pollution and then apply the content, she or he can conduct a quick search for "classroom activities on air pollution." Such a search generates many online worksheets, activities, experiments, etc. For those who are tech-savvy or who want to record their own lectures, advances in technology and online recording programs have made it easier to record lectures. Video content does not need to be long; in most cases, videos of between 5 and 15 minutes are recommended.

PART 3—STRATEGIES

Flipping without Technology

Flipping with Your Textbook

A common belief about flipped learning is that it must involve technology, notably that the instructor videotapes his or her own lectures or presentations of the content for students to watch at home. This does happen a lot, but ESL teachers should be afforded some latitude for two reasons. First, ESL classes often are not lecture-type classes. It isn't likely that an instructor is going to prepare a 50-minute or 75-minute lecture on the activating-your-prior-knowledge before-reading strategy or the narrowing-your-topic strategy before students begin researching and writing a paper. Those skills are condensed into content boxes (or the like) and often provide examples. It would be challenging to convert this into a formal lecture. Second, much of ESL course content is covered in the published textbooks. Why stop using the textbooks so carefully selected for the students? The material in the textbooks is sound and teaches what instructors need it to teach. Instructors could record their own, if they wish; videos need not be class-length lectures (see page 37).

Think about your own teaching style and your own classroom. In general, instructors require students to bring their book to class. The class covers whatever pages were planned for that day and students complete the exercises, and then the instructor assigns something as homework. Starting to flip in these cases can really be quite easy. Why not have students read the pages at home, do some or all the activities at home, compare and check answers in class, and then write, read, practice, and interact in class when everyone is together? Similarly, depending on the level of the class, instructors may just ask students to read the pages at home. To begin flipping, the instructor can ask the students to complete the activities with a partner or with a small group and then work on the given assignment. This plan results in a more interactive class or certainly one in which the students work and make progress at their own individual level.

For each of the following examples (Figures 15–17), a brief look at a possible "traditional" lesson is given along with a possible way to begin flipping. Bear in mind that there is nothing wrong with the traditional approach.

The first example is from a writing textbook (*Inside Academic Writing*) in a unit that covers problem-solution writing. The Describing a Solution task is presented, and a sample is provided. Process words are also included. Finally, a writing assignment is given (see Figure 15). The comparison of a traditional versus a flipped lesson follows (see page 42).

Figure 15. Example of Writing Content and Assignment Ideal for a Problem-Solution Lesson

Describing a Solution

When presenting the solution for either a research or technical problem, you need to describe the process or the steps for implementing the solution—either how the solution can be implemented or how it has been applied. This information has to flow clearly, so another scientist can follow the process and replicate the steps. Notice the flow of information in the solution section of "Gas-Fueled Tools Can Poison Users" from *Impact on Construction Safety and Health,* Vol. 13, No. 1, May 1995). Also notice **bolded** passive voice verb forms in the text. Process texts usually contain passive forms because the person (or subject) who performs the process is not important.

■ ■ ■ ■ ■ ■ ■ ■ ■ ■ ■ ■ ■ ■ ■ ■ ■ ■ ■ ■

Gas-Fueled Tools Can Poison Users

The risk of carbon monoxide poisoning can be cut by using electric or diesel equipment, good ventilation, monitoring, and training. But you need to make sure the solution doesn't add new problems. Electrical equipment should have a ground-fault circuit interrupter to lower the chance of electrocution. Diesel-fueled equipment **needs to be properly fitted** with filters for diesel particulates in the air that can probably cause cancer. Diesel- and gas-fueled equipment **should also be fitted** with a catalytic converter and well-maintained, to give off less carbon monoxide. Even with these steps, the amount of carbon monoxide may still be too high to use the equipment in some areas. Air monitoring **is needed** to make sure workers are not exposed to unsafe levels of the gas. This monitoring requires special equipment and people trained to use it. Contractors and all workers **must also be told** about the dangers of using gas-fueled equipment in enclosed spaces. Warning labels **can be used.** Training can show how to use the equipment safely.

afterward	eventually	last
at last	finally	later
at the same time	first of all	meanwhile
before this	formerly	previously
currently	initially	simultaneously
during	in the future	

Also, be careful not to overuse the common words *and, next, or first* repeatedly when describing the steps; use any of the variety of words that signal a process listed.

Exercise 8F: Writing a Short Summary

Write a short summary about a process you used to complete a lab experiment, a piece of writing, or any other task that interests you. First, list the steps in the process. Then combine the steps into a paragraph that flows well. Avoid common words (*and, next,* or *first*) by using signal markers from the box. Write in the passive voice, so the focus is on the process and not the person performing the process.

From: Canseco. (2010). *Inside Academic Writing,* pages 143–144, University of Michigan Press.

Traditional	Flipped
In Class: Present the introductory passage about solutions. Review the example and signal words. Give students time to read the example again if needed. Answer any questions. **Homework:** Ask students to complete the writing assignment (8F) (writing a short summary).	**Homework:** Ask students to read the passage in the textbook. **In Class:** Begin a writing workshop in which students write and submit their own short summary. In another flipped session, hold a peer review period in which students read and comment on their peers' summaries, allowing for revision before the final submission to the instructor.

The next example is a writing strategy from the *Four Point* series (see Figure 16). The comparison of a traditional versus a flipped version follows (see page 47).

Figure 16. Example of Content on Paraphrasing for an EAP Lesson

Writing Strategy: Paraphrasing, Part 1

Paraphrasing is rewriting ideas from a secondary source. Paraphrases are challenging because they are written using different words, but they need to retain the meaning of the original. Paraphrases are approximately the same length as the original. It is good to learn to paraphrase in order to avoid plagiarism. Plagiarism is using other writers' ideas and words without acknowledging them.

There are several ways that you can paraphrase. You must use more than one when you are paraphrasing.

These techniques focus on changing words or phrases.

- **Replace words with synonyms**

  Original: *Given the odds, such a bold commitment was, at the time, outrageous.*

  One example with synonyms: *Given the chances, such a daring promise was, at the time, shocking.*

Remember that highly specialized or technical words can remain unchanged.

- **Shorten longer words or phrases**

  Original: *Given the odds, such a bold commitment was, at the time, outrageous.*

  One example with shortened words or phrases: *Odds were, such a commitment was, then, outrageous.*

- **Lengthen shorter words or phrases**

  Original: *Given the odds, such a bold commitment was, at the time, outrageous.*

  One example with lengthened words or phrases: *Given the odds, a commitment that bold was, at the time of delivery, outrageous.*

- **Change the part of speech of words**

  Original: *Given the odds, such a bold commitment was, at the time, outrageous.*

  One example with changed parts of speech: *Given the odds, committing so boldly was, at the time, outrageously shocking.*

- **Add words**

  Original: *Given the odds, such a bold commitment was, at the time, outrageous.*

  One example with added words: *With the odds, such a bold commitment was, during Kennedy's time, completely outrageous.*

Using just one of these techniques <u>does not</u> change the original enough to avoid plagiarism. Combine them with each other. You also still need to cite the source.

Original: *Given the odds, such a bold commitment was, at the time, outrageous.*

One example with more than one strategy: *Considering the situation, a daring promise like that was, then, quite shocking (Collins, 1997).*

Practice Activity: Paraphrasing

Rewrite the words or phrases using each of the paraphrasing strategies.

1. Replace words with synonyms

   excellent _____

   missions _____

2. Shorten longer words or phrases

   achieving the goal _____

   before this decade is out _____

3. Lengthen shorter words or phrases

compelling in its own right _____

easily understood by everyone _____

4. Change the parts of speech of words

different _____

compelling _____

5. Add words

It engages people—it reaches out and grabs them in the gut.

_____

_____

People "get it" right away; it takes little or no explanation.

_____

_____

6. Go back to the Paraphrasing to Simplify exercise, and answer these questions.

a. Did you use any of these strategies? Which ones? _____

_____

b. Where can you use more than one? _____

c. Can you edit the paraphrases you wrote? Mark places in your paraphrases where you think you can make changes.

d. Can you write one completely new paraphrase?

_____

_____

_____

_____

_____

_____

_____

Short Writing Tasks

Write your response to each task following the directions given for length and source material.

Task 1 (Summary)

Look again at Reading 1. Write a one-paragraph paraphrase of Paragraph 2. Try to use the paraphrasing strategies from this unit. Review the box on pages 14–15. (Length: 4–6 sentences)

Task 2 (Research)

Reading 1 talks about mission statements. Based on your instructor's guidelines, do some light research online or in a library. Light research is not as detailed and does not take as much time as preparation for a long essay or research paper. Light research includes finding a few sources that provide some supporting details. Find an example of a mission statement from your school or one of its departments. You may also choose to find a mission statement for another school or university. Write the mission statement, where it is from, and describe how it fits (or doesn't fit) the characteristics described in Reading 1. Take notes in the space provided. Then write your paragraph on a separate piece of paper. (Length: 5–7 sentences)

From Lockwood & Sippell. (2012). *Four Point Reading and Writing Intro*, pages 14–18, University of Michigan Press.

Traditional	Flipped
In Class: Define paraphrasing and present the strategies (see Figure 16). Give students time to work on the practice activity. Share answers. **Homework:** Ask students to complete one or both of the Short Writing Tasks for formal submission on a given date (see Figure 16).	**Homework:** Ask students to read the strategy box and complete the practice activity. **In Class:** Share answers and ideas. Give students time to write other answers and ideas in their textbook since there are a variety of correct answers. Complete one or both of the short writing tasks and submit a rough draft before class ends.

Another example from the same book could have several flipped models (see page 49) depending on whether an instructor wants students to read outside of class or practice the strategy together while reading in class. This example uses the During Reading Strategy, Annotating as You Read (Figure 17).

Figure 17. Example of Reading Content Ideal for Flipping

During Reading Strategy: Annotating as You Read

Annotating is basically summarizing the most important information in each paragraph as you read by making notes. You cannot summarize without understanding what you've read, so it is a useful way to check comprehension. In addition, you are creating a useful study guide that you can use to participate during class discussions and to study for tests. You can write your notes in the margin or on sticky notes. You can also circle, highlight, or underline main ideas and definitions.

You might want to note the purpose of some paragraphs; for example, you could mark a story used to explain a point as "example" or "ex." An example of how Paragraph 1 of Reading 2 could be annotated is shown.

The fundamental distinguishing characteristic of the most enduring and successful corporations is that they preserve a (cherished) *valued* core ideology while simultaneously stimulating progress and change in everything that is not part of their core ideology. Put another way, they distinguish their timeless core values and enduring core purpose (which should never change) from their operating practices and business strategies (which should be changing constantly in response to a changing world). In truly great companies, change *is* a constant, but not the *only* constant. They understand the difference between what should never change and what should be open for change, between what is truly (sacred) and what is not. And by being clear about what should never change, they are better able to stimulate change and progress in everything else.

Margin notes:

fund char.—keep core ideology, start progress

value & purpose—never change

strategies—always changing

great companies know the diff.

sacred = something held dear, same as cherished

From Lockwood & Sippell. (2012). *Four Point Reading and Writing Intro*, page 22, University of Michigan Press.

Traditional

In Class: Present the During Reading Strategy. Make sure students understand the example. Give students time to complete the associated practice activity (Figure 17) before reading. Review the answers.

Homework: Ask students to read the reading passage and to annotate as they read. Prepare students to turn in their annotations on the given date.

Flipped 1	Flipped 2
Homework: Ask students to read the During Reading Strategy and then to complete the practice activity. **In Class:** Compare annotations from the practice activity. Give students time to discuss what was easy and worked well for them and what they found more difficult. Allow time for students to read the reading passage and annotate as they read.	**Homework:** Ask students to read the During Reading Strategy and to complete the practice and vocabulary activities. Ask students to read and annotate the reading passage. **In Class:** Compare annotations from the practice activity and for the reading. Hold small group discussions in which students discuss what worked and didn't work well for them. Using a textbook for another class or a reading passage of interest to each individual student, ask them to annotate and then make a copy to submit.

Flipping Doesn't Require Creative Genius

Using the Extra Material in Textbooks

Often, one of the biggest concerns in flipping the ESL classroom is the amount of time it takes to plan activities to fill the class time. Instructors may feel overwhelmed because they were accustomed to covering material in the books or presenting whatever content was necessary in the limited amount of class time available. The impression that some instructors have is that flipping requires them to abandon what they were doing and create new activities and plans, which seems like a frightening proposition.

The benefits detailed in Part 2 often sway many instructors into trying a flipped model. Many instructors want more interactive classes that are actually fun to teach and fun for the students rather than just a simple recitation of the content. Flipping allows ESL students to see class as useful and interactive more than as a necessary evil. Although instructors likely have a lot of their own material that they've developed and collected, it isn't necessary to sift through boxes and boxes of materials collected over the years. It doesn't need to be that hard. What does one really need to do to attempt flipping?

Start gradually! In some cases, only a set of discussion questions is needed. Some short group activities followed by a sharing session with the whole class work as well. As long as the students are applying the content or "doing the homework" in class, then that is enough work for many ESL settings, at least as a starting point. In some of these cases, the textbooks themselves have material. Material that you previously didn't have time for or that had been assigned as homework can now be used as the classroom material. Some can even be easily converted into a group project if not already designed that way.

Figure 18 shows an example of a group discussion provided in a textbook in the *Four Point* series. When teaching in a traditional model, the videos and audio are played in class and may require extra time if they need to be played more than once. In this example, students watch the video that accompanies the textbook outside of class. The time dedicated to audio and visual generally detracts from the ability to use these discussion activities or other materials provided within the unit. If they are used, students are forced to complete them outside of class. They must find time to meet each other and juggle this activity without the guidance of the instructor. A flipped model allows more time for the group interaction in class with guidance provided as needed. Students have the opportunity to cover more material in the book, practice more, and actually apply what they've learned while using higher-order and critical-thinking skills.

Figure 18. Example of Discussion Activity for Flipping an EAP Lesson

Discussion

In the video, the students brainstormed and expressed which ideas they liked and why. They also admitted a lack of information when they couldn't remember the details. Being able to have strong reasons for what you consider to be a priority and being able to professionally reject others' ideas is an important skill to master in academic discussions.

Imagine you are a team of astronomers who have discovered a new planet in the solar system. You believe there is life on this new planet and the inhabitants of such a planet are very different from Earthlings. Brainstorm a list of attributes that these new people have.

Attributes of the Inhabitants of the New Planet

_____

_____

_____

_____

_____

You've now been told by your boss at NASA that not all of the attributes should be announced in the first press release about the discovery. Work with your team to choose only three attributes to include in the press release. Be prepared to explain why you've selected these three items for inclusion.

Our Top Three

_____

_____

_____

From: Folse & Lockwood. (2010). *Four Point Listening and Speaking 1*, page 223, University of Michigan Press.

A similar model can be used for the exercises shown in Figure 19. These exercises are from the grammar textbook, *Clear Grammar 2, 2nd edition*. Like many grammar textbooks, a wealth of exercises are provided so students can practice the grammar points being taught. Often there are so many that some may have to be skipped simply because there isn't enough class time. Instructors may skip the speaking or writing exercises because there isn't time and those involve students using more than just the grammar skill being taught. However, if a flipped approach is adopted, at least in part, many of the exercises are done as homework rather than in class. The speaking practice, which is more interactive, is then used to fill the now-free class time. The writing practice can also be done in class and the writing can be submitted before students leave, thus preventing them from having what they would call "homework." Students use higher-order skills and apply the grammar to something besides rote exercises.

Figure 19. Example of Grammar Exercise for Flipping

Speaking Practice: Interviewing Classmates

First write your answers to the questions. Then work with a partner. Take turns interviewing each other. Pay attention to verb tenses in your answers. Ask your partner these questions:

1. What did you do last weekend?

_____

_____

2. Think of someone who is not here in this class. What do you think that person is doing right now?

_____

_____

3. What are your plans for next weekend? What are you going to do?

_____

_____

4. What are two of your hobbies? How long have you done these activities?

_____

_____

Original Student Writing

Write several sentences about people in your family. Use each of these tenses at least once in your work: simple present, present progressive, simple past, **be going to,** and present perfect.

From: Folse, (2012). *Clear Grammar 2, 2nd Edition*, pages 35 and 43, University of Michigan Press.

Using the Instructor's Manuals

When instructors begin to add flipping to their courses, they may not have a lot of their own activities prepared. In today's world, there are so many other ideas and materials already developed that instructors don't have to rely solely on their own ideas. Take advantage of other people's ideas. Colleagues at universities who are generous may share their activities from their own fields (the very fields students will eventually be studying in), and colleagues across the world in ESL are also generous and share ideas. Also, news sources, such as *The New York Times* or CNN, government agencies, and educational institutions provide resources. So much is already out there.

Don't forget that a lot of legwork has already been done by the publishers. Instructor's manuals often include ideas that work well for a flipped classroom. Consider reviewing the instructor's manuals that accompany your textbooks for ideas to implement in a flipped ESL classroom. Often these are directly related to the content, are more interactive, utilize authentic materials, require higher-order skills, or include ideas for group or pair work, all of which are ideal in a flipped classroom setting. Look for subject headings such as Expansion Activities, Extension Activities, Optional Activities, Reproducible Worksheets, and other key words to identify activities for the classroom.

Figure 20 is an example from the reading-writing strand of the *Four Point* series. A pre-reading strategy is taught and followed by a practice activity (see Figure 20). Various amounts of material are covered in a traditional classroom. More than likely, the reading strategy box is presented, the practice activity completed, and perhaps even the reading is done in class. Depending on class time, the reading may be assigned as homework. In some cases, perhaps even the practice activity is done as homework (with the reading done in the next class or as part of the homework). If some of these activities, however, are completed at home in a flipped classroom model, then there is class time available for more interactive work, the incorporation of outside sources, and some activity that requires students to apply the material and use higher-order skills. The instructor's manual for this strategy box provides such an activity (see Figure 21).

Figure 20. Example of Reading Content/Practice to Flip

Before Reading Strategy: Preparing for a New Topic

Imagine that you have been assigned a reading that is on a topic that is new to you and outside your area of expertise. Read the title of the reading. Before you even start reading, you recognize that you are worried that you won't understand enough of the vocabulary to be able to understand the reading. What can you do?

1. Go online or to a reference book and try to find a short explanation of the topic or event. In the case of Reading 2, it might be "structural engineering." In this type of source, the explanation is designed to be simple and general. It will give you a basic idea of the concepts and vocabulary. It might also provide some ideas for similar topics you could look at. Make a list of words on the topic that might appear in the reading.

2. Go online to look for photos related to the topic of the reading. Sometimes you just need to be able to get a picture in your head of a particular concept. In the case of Reading 2, look again at the photos, but also search for photos online related to the building of the Hoover Dam.

3. Skim the reading to look for vocabulary that you don't know. Make a list of the words and add them to your vocabulary log. Look up the meanings <u>before</u> you start reading. See the Vocabulary Strategy.

4. Skim the reading to look for other clues to understanding what the reading is about. Talk to your classmates. Share what you think you know.

Practice: Preparing for a New Topic

Prepare for the reading by answering these questions.

1. Look up "structural engineering" in a reference book or online source. What is given as the basic meaning?

   _____

   _____

2. As you read more about the topic, what are some vocabulary words that you see used more than once?

   _____

   _____

3. Skim the reading to see if you find any of the same words in the reading. If so, which ones?

   _____

   _____

4. Write a sentence about what you think the reading will be about.

   _____

   _____

From: Lockwood & Sippell. (2012). *Four Point Reading and Writing Intro*, pages 55–56, University of Michigan Press.

Figure 21. Example of Activity from Instructor's Manual

Expansion Activity

Many students will rely on online sources. Consider a brief discussion about reliable sources. Go over the classroom policy as well as any university policies. For example, some instructors do not consider Wikipedia a reliable source. Discuss types of websites and generate a discussion about which are reliable. A list is included.

.gov
.edu
.org
.com
.net
.mil

Compare and contrast sources such as blogs, social networking sites, or news sources, and also consider comparing and contrasting print versus online sources. A review of comparing and contrasting language is in *Four Point Listening and Speaking Intro* (Unit 2).

Put students in small groups to look at the list of sites they used and/or have them brainstorm a list of reliable sources for each type of website. Create a master list on the board for students to copy and use as they move forward through the *Four Point* series.

From: Instructor's Manual to accompany *Four Point Reading and Writing Intro* (2012).

The flipped model allows some flexibility and can be adapted based on how much class time is available. Perhaps the practice activity in Figure 20 could be done in class in groups before students participate in the Expansion Activity provided in the instructor's manual. Then, students could do the reading in class. This seems counterintuitive in that many instructors ask students to do the reading at home, but flipping allows the instructor to be there to make sure the reading strategy is practiced. Students often perceive this as "no homework" because they don't have as much to read outside of class, which helps get student buy-in. Instructors can continue to expand activities in a flipped classroom and/or let students compare answers for whatever work was completed at home. For example, instructors can ask students to create a list of reliable sources for another course or a field of interest to them. If a student wants to study medicine, she or he might compile a list including prominent hospital sites like the Mayo Clinic, organizations such as the American Medical Association, the Society for Pediatric Radiology, or the World Health Organization, or general information and government sites such as WebMD, healthfinder.gov, or the National Institutes of Health (nih.gov). Similarly, if students are studying related fields, this can be completed in a group.

Many instructors spend time creating puzzles and activities to use as homework. However, a lot of ancillary products have done the legwork already. These can just as easily be used in a flipped classroom. Figure 22 shows a vocabulary box from a reading textbook, *Challenges 1: Reading and Vocabulary for Academic Success*. The word chart is followed by several different activities, such as matching and sentence completion. Traditionally, class time can be filled with completing the chart, working on a variety of provided activities, and going over answers. The reproducible activities provided online for instructors (see Figure 23) are likely to be assigned as homework if used at all, especially if the reading is assigned as well. Instead, flip the classroom. Use these activities in class. The puzzle can be done as a competitive race to see which individual or group finishes first. The Topics for Further Discussion might actually be discussed rather than skipped. They require critical thinking about the topic and are not simply comprehension questions. The Your Reading Journal activity can be done in class rather than assigned as homework. Ask students to share their similes (or give them time to write in class where they can solicit help and share ideas from peers).

Figure 22. Example of Vocabulary Activity to Flip

Vocabulary Comprehension

With a classmate, fill in the empty boxes in the chart. Do not write anything in the boxes that have an X. You can use an English dictionary.

Nouns	Verbs	Adjectives	Adverbs
	accumulate		X
1. 2.	derive		X
	relax	X	
	require	X	
X	seek	X	X
vehicle	X		X
	warn	X	X

From: Boardman & Barton. (2012). *Challenges 1: Reading and Vocabulary for Academic Success*, page 42, University of Michigan Press.

Figure 23. Examples of Vocabulary and Discussion Activities to Flip

D	S	N	R	T	U	S	U	O	R	E	N	E	G	T
E	P	U	I	R	E	Q	W	E	R	B	N	M	S	H
P	W	E	I	G	H	Y	Z	F	H	R	T	I	R	Z
R	Y	M	E	S	E	B	O	C	D	G	S	V	E	E
E	A	C	C	U	M	U	L	A	T	E	P	O	Q	V
S	R	E	T	Y	D	E	N	E	R	G	Y	Y	U	I
S	B	D	E	R	I	V	E	L	A	N	K	U	I	T
E	R	N	I	V	E	N	T	I	R	E	X	O	R	C
D	E	X	Z	E	E	V	M	R	S	L	E	K	E	E
K	G	V	I	H	K	E	E	S	D	L	X	Q	G	P
U	R	F	P	I	R	B	K	P	F	A	C	G	H	S
Y	E	D	T	C	Y	N	W	K	L	H	E	M	J	R
T	T	R	W	L	Y	M	I	E	G	C	S	B	K	E
R	E	K	A	E	K	P	R	J	H	B	S	L	O	P
W	A	R	N	S	I	N	F	I	N	I	T	E	L	Y

Topics for Further Discussion

In small groups, discuss these questions.

1. The French word *flaneur* means a person who experiences a city by walking in it. What do you like and dislike about walking in cities?

2. Walking tour companies offer group and private walking tours of cities, towns, and natural places around the world. If you could design your own walking tour, where would you go?

3. In the Macua culture of Africa, people say that, "Walking in two is medicine." Explain what this means. Do you agree with this idea?

Your Reading Journal

In a Reading Journal, you have the chance to write your thoughts about a topic. Because a Reading Journal is informal, you can practice expressing your thoughts and ideas freely. You can also practice English structures you're studying.

Write similes using these phrases.

1. as noisy as . . .

2. as bright as . . .

3. as soft as . . .

4. as exciting as . . .

5. as heavy as . . .

Use metaphors to describe these things or ideas.

1. Your eyes are . . .

2. A baby's skin is . . .

3. Freshly baked cookies are . . .

4. Friendship is . . .

5. Stars are . . .

From: Online activities to accompany *Challenges 1: Reading and Vocabulary for Academic Success* (2012). University of Michigan Press.

Using "Everyday" ESL Activities

In so many classes, when teaching any of the main skills (listening, speaking, reading, and writing) or the language bases (grammar and vocabulary), all instructors use some activities that are "everyday" or common, such as role-plays or debates. These can be applied to material with a specific book, but they can also be applied to materials from other books, lectures from textbooks or websites played for listening classes, or any other material to give the flipped classroom that interactive nature. Perhaps they weren't used as often as they could have been since time is often an issue, but some of that time is gained back in a flipped classroom. Or perhaps a debate wasn't used because it wasn't a speaking class, but that is no longer an issue in a flipped classroom. The focus shifts to the interactive nature, the use of content, and the use of higher-order skills. Debates and other "everyday" activities can be used more readily.

The Instructor's Manual for *Thinking Critically: World Issues for Reading, Writing, and Research* offers some general debate and role-play guidelines that can be used with every unit of the book (see Figures 24 and 25). Additionally, instructor's manuals might give specific ideas for how to incorporate those general guidelines to specific content in the textbook that you are using.

Although these guidelines were written for one particular textbook, they could be applied generally to debate or role-play activities for listening passages in other books or to any other content in which students are expected to be able to discuss, comprehend, synthesize, critique, evaluate, and analyze. Additionally, many books offer their own guidelines specific to their text material or guidelines that can be adapted to suit your flipped classroom.

Figure 26 (pages 66–68) shows an example of a debate format in the *Four Point* series (*Listening and Speaking 1*).

Figure 24. Example of Debate Guidelines

Debate

In a debate, two teams present opposing arguments on a controversial topic with the goal of convincing the audience of their point of view. The Pro team presents arguments in favor of a topic. The Con team presents arguments in opposition to a topic. Each team has a leader who gives an opening statement and a closing statement. The team members prepare questions and answers on the topic.

Debate Guidelines
- Each team has approximately the same number of members.
- Each team elects a leader.
- All members of the team are prepared to speak at least once and to give a rebuttal (answering argument) to the opposing team's statements.
- No one person dominates the debate; all team members contribute equally to the debate.
- The person who is speaking is not interrupted.

Debate Format
- Pro team introductory statement (5 minutes)
- Con team introductory statement (5minutes)
- Con team questions and pro team answers (15 minutes)
- Pro team questions and con team answers (15 minutes)
- Con team concluding statement (5 minutes)
- Pro team concluding statement (5 minutes)

Debate Preparation
- Do Internet and library research to locate relevant information on the debate topic.
- List your team's major arguments in order of strength.
- List questions you think the opposing team will ask, and write down your responses.
- Write down questions your team will ask the opposing team.
- Summarize your team's strongest arguments.

Debate Evaluation

Excellent +   **Satisfactory √**   **Unsatisfactory −**

Evaluate the members of the opposite team as excellent, satisfactory, or unsatisfactory, according to the following criteria.

- Participation: All members of the team participated by making statements, asking questions of the other team, or answering the other team's questions. ____

- Organization: The team began with introductions of its members and ended with a clear closing statement. ____

- Presentation: The team members communicated their position persuasively by combining delivery, gestures, and eye contact to create an image of competence. ____

- Analysis: The team presented the strongest possible arguments to support its position. ____

- Evidence: The team supported its arguments with good examples and substantial evidence. ____

- Questions: The team's questions were concise and exposed weaknesses in the opposing team's arguments. ____

- Answers: The team's answers to questions were concise, to the point, and logically supportive of their team's position. ____

- Approach: The team treated the opposing team with respect, consideration, and fairness. ____

Overall Evaluation _____

Comments

From: Instructor's Manual to accompany *Thinking Critically: World Issues for Reading, Writing, and Research, Second Edition* (2014). University of Michigan Press.

Figure 25. Example of Role-Play Guidelines

Role Play

In a role play, students act out a realistic situation. Performing a role play is an excellent way in which to improve listening and speaking skills. A role play can also increase communicative skills. The following guidelines help you to plan, practice, and present a role play.

- Work in teams of two or three. The third person serves as a coach to help the two actors prepare and rehearse the role play (unless a third person is needed for the role play).
- Discuss the role play scenarios with your partner(s), choose your role, and reread the instructions.
- Develop several objectives for your role play, and put them in writing.
- Think about your character and plan what your character will say.
  - Make notes about the broad ideas and emotions you will act out.
  - Decide how to achieve your objectives for the role play.
- Rehearse the role play with your partner.
  - Do not try to write out the dialogue.
  - Let your dialogue develop naturally and spontaneously.
- Present the role play to the class. (It should be about 5 minutes long.)
  - Speak in a loud and clear voice, and don't be afraid to exaggerate your actions.
  - Listen carefully to what your partner is saying before you respond.
  - Pay attention to nonverbal communication signals of eye contact, facial expressions, gestures, and body language.
- Discuss the issues seen in the role play with the class afterward.
  - What reactions did your classmates have?
  - Were your objectives achieved?

Negotiation

In a negotiation, two opposing teams discuss issues in order to arrive at an agreement that is fair and acceptable to both sides. You will work with a team to plan, prepare, and participate in a negotiation session. Each student has to decide whether to be a member of Team A, from India, or Team B, from Pakistan.

Negotiation Guidelines

- Choose a team leader.
- Decide whether to use collaborative bargaining (a rather friendly approach) or adversarial bargaining (a somewhat hostile approach).
- Draw up a list of issues for the negotiating sessions.
- Put the issues in order of priority.
- Limit the negotiation session to 15 minutes.
- Critique your classmates' negotiating skills after the negotiation session.

Negotiation Format

- India team introductory statement (5 minutes)
- Pakistan team introductory statement (5minutes)
- India team issues (20 minutes)
- Pakistan team issues (20 minutes)
- India team concluding statement (5 minutes)
- Pakistan team concluding statement (5 minutes)

Negotiation Preparation

- Prioritize the major issues that must be resolved.
- List your team's positions on these issues: your ideal solution.
- Write down the supporting arguments for your team's positions.
- Write down the compromise positions that your team would accept if necessary: your bottom line.
- Practice your negotiation style: collaborative bargaining or adversarial bargaining.

From: Instructor's Manual to accompany *Thinking Critically: World Issues for Reading, Writing, and Research, Second Edition* (2014). University of Michigan Press.

Figure 26. Example of Debate Format Adaptable to Any Level

Debate

Divide the class into two teams. One team will discuss the pros to working for a large, established company (and the cons to being an entrepreneur). The other team will discuss the pros to entrepreneurship (and the cons to working for a large, established company).

Topic: Entrepreneurship

Pro or Con: _____

Choose one team member to give an introductory statement and one to give a closing statement. Divide the arguments evenly among the remaining team members. You will need to be prepared to disagree, and counter at least one point from the other team. Each statement, argument, and counterargument lasts for two minutes.

Follow this debate format:

> Pro team member gives an introductory statement on the topic to present/preview pro opinion
>
> Con team gives an introductory statement on the topic to present/preview con opinion
>
> Con team member delivers first argument
>
> Pro team member rebuts with counterargument
>
> Pro team member delivers next argument
>
> Con team member rebuts with counterargument
>
> Team members will continue exchanging arguments and rebuttals until all team members have delivered their arguments and counterarguments.
>
> Open discussion (10 minutes)
>
> Pro team member gives a closing statement/summary on pro team's argument
>
> Con team member gives a closing statement/summary on con team's argument

Team member giving introductory statement _____

Team member giving closing statement _____

Other arguments: _____

_____

_____

_____

_____

_____

Preparing Individually

Think about the selected topic and then write two reasons that support your business type and two that are against your business type. You need to think about both sides so that you can argue effectively against the other team.

Pro 1:

_____

_____

_____

Pro 2:

_____

_____

_____

Con 1:

_____

_____

_____

Con 2:

_____

_____

_____

Preparing as a Group

Now work with your team. Take turns discussing your pros and cons. Your group should select the strongest pros and cons to use during the debate. Select arguments that you think will be difficult for the other team to disagree with. Also think about responses you can use to counter the other team's arguments.

Arguments:

_____

_____

_____

_____

_____

_____

_____

_____

Counterarguments:

_____

_____

_____

_____

_____

_____

_____

_____

From: Folse & Lockwood. (2010). *Four Point Listening and Speaking 1*, pages 111–113, University of Michigan Press.

Figure 27 presents examples of dictation and a grammar practice that are also tried and true for any level. They seem to work well in a flipped classroom setting and are easy to find or develop. Additionally, practicing grammar in the classroom rather than at home allows time for the instructor to answer specific questions in the guide-on-the-side fashion rather than students trying to apply the rules or ideas on their own.

We may all question our own creativity, but seeing a lot of these ideas may allow us to apply them to other content or even inspire new ideas.

Figure 27. Example of Dictation Adaptable for Any Level

Dictation

Dictation involves every student in active learning. It provides great practice and requires few materials. It can be used to introduce content, practice content being learned, or review learned content. It can be used for assessment. This teacher's guide for each unit contains dictation sentences. The sentences are sometimes open-ended where the student writes the dictated prompt and then fills it in with personal information. Other dictations are complete sentences. The dictations reuse the important vocabulary from the reading so the students have a chance to meet the words again. The dictations can be used on the day following the reading as a follow-up activity or on the day preceding the reading as a prior knowledge activity.

Prepositions

A preposition is a word used in front of a noun or pronoun to show the location, the position in time, or some other relationship between the noun or pronoun object and another word or words in the sentence. Prepositions are most commonly used to show positions in time or space. Although there are more than 100 prepositions, only about 30 are commonly used. Of these, nine prepositions account for 92 percent of all preposition usage. These nine are, in order of use: *of, to, in, for, on, with, by, at, from.* Each unit in Book 3 works on one of these prepositions.

Students make three kinds of errors with prepositions: They use a preposition where it is not needed, they leave out a preposition where it is needed, or they use the wrong preposition. Practice using prepositions will help students feel more comfortable using prepositions in sentences and understanding prepositions in print.

Activities

- Circle the prepositions in sentences.
- Write two sentences using specified prepositions.
- Complete the sentences with prepositional phrases.
- Fill in the blanks with prepositions.
- Match a preposition to an adjective and noun.
- Play a preposition Pictionary game. A student selects a card with a preposition on it. The student then draws a picture on the board to indicate that preposition so the classmates can guess it. For example, for the word *in*, students could draw a cat in a box or a man in a car.
- Give students maps and ask them to locate places on the map. "_____ is on _____ street, next to the _____."
- Ask students to draw a picture incorporating specified elements (e.g., a large car, a tall tree, a house with a large window and a door, etc). Now give the students a preposition and ask them to draw something in their picture using that preposition. (For example, with the preposition *above*, students might draw a cloud over the house or a bird above the tree.) After several items have been completed, students can share their pictures with classmates and write sentences describing their use of the prepositions.
- Ask the students to find a paragraph from an article in the newspaper or a magazine, and underline all of the prepositional phrases.
- Ask students to describe objects in a room in their house using five prepositional phrases.
- Whiteboards are an excellent way to work with prepositions. Students can easily draw, change, or add objects on white boards, and they can also add or change the objects of prepositions in sentences.

From: Instructor's Manual to accompany *What's Up 3: Integrated Skills and Culture* (2009). University of Michigan Press.

Using Authentic Materials in Class

Other Textbooks or Reading Material

A flipped classroom allows inclusion of more authentic materials. Students often like what they call "real" material because they see what they're being taught transferring to material outside the ESL classroom. Each may define "real" differently. For example, if they can transfer their skills to textbooks in their general education or graduate-level classes, then the skills are appealing to them. Other times they may want to see the skills as useful in professional or life-skills settings. Flipped classrooms allow for this much more readily than traditional classrooms that are more focused on only what is in the textbook or delivered during a lecture.

When I teach using the material in the *Four Point* series, I have a head start. The readings are from other textbooks and authentic academic materials. However, often students still view this as ESL and it can be challenging for them to see the connection to using this on textbooks in their other courses. Traditionally, an instructor likely presents the strategy and assigns the practice activity and the reading as homework. Figure 28 provides an example of a reading strategy that accompanies an excerpt from a novel and its accompanying practice activity.

Rather than spending time on this in class, students can do much of this on their own at home. Discussion that requires higher-level skills such as analysis, evaluation, or synthesis can be done in class: What did students like about this strategy? Did it work? What answers do they have for the practice activity? With what other types of material can they use this skill? The bulk of class time can be dedicated to the Expansion Activity from the instructor's manual (see Figure 29). This lets students do homework for another class (or at least relate it to a field in which they are interested), increasing the chance that they will value it more.

Figure 28. Example of Reading Content and Practice for Flipping

During Reading Strategy: Asking Questions as You Read

A helpful strategy used by good readers of academic content is asking themselves questions as they read. The important part of this strategy is to ask questions, not thinking about the type of questions you ask. Asking questions not only keeps you focused on the topic, but it keeps you engaged with the content. Staying engaged will better enable you to finish the reading with some level of understanding.

In academic reading, questions can help you check your level of understanding, particularly if you are reading something that is unfamiliar to you, and especially when reading fiction or about fiction.

Ask yourself important questions about the details. In fiction, ask yourself about the setting, the characters, and the time. For example, this is the first paragraph from the novel *The Good Earth*:

> It was Wang Lung's marriage day. At first, opening his eyes in the blackness of the curtains about his bed, he could not think why the dawn seemed different from any other. The house was still except for the faint, gasping cough of his old father, whose room was opposite to his own across the middle room. Every morning the old man's cough was the first sound to be heard. Wang Lung usually lay listening to it and moved only when he heard it approaching nearer and when he heard the door of his father's room squeak upon its wooden hinges.

Based only on this paragraph, the questions you might ask are:

- **Do I know who all the characters are?**
- **Do I understand how they are related?**

Practice Activity: Asking Questions as You Read

Notice the STOP signs in the margin of Reading 1. These are placed throughout the reading to remind you to stop and check your comprehension at key points. When you get to each STOP sign, stop reading and answer the questions about each section.

SECTION 1

1. Who are the main characters and what did you learn about them?

   _____

2. When and where is the story set?

   _____

SECTION 2

1. Why was *The Good Earth* an important novel in the U.S.?

   _____

SECTION 3

1. What was happening in China's history at the time the novel is set?

   _____

SECTION 4

1. What literary style is *The Good Earth?* Why?

   _____

SECTION 5

1. What is important about the author's knowledge of or experience in China?

   _____

THE END

Now that you have read the reading in its entirety, what do you think are the most important pieces of information for understanding the reading?

_____
_____

From: Lockwood & Sippell. (2012). *Four Point Reading and Writing Intro*, pages 200–201, University of Michigan Press.

Figure 29. Example of Activity Suited for Flipping a Reading Lesson

Expansion Activity

Assign a day for students to bring a textbook from another class or a piece of reading they need for research or are interested in. Repeat the activity in the box and ask students to read the first paragraph of the reading they chose and write several yes-no questions to accompany the material.

From: Instructor's Manual to accompany *Four Point Reading and Writing Intro* (2012).

Realia

Having a flipped classroom allows instructors to better differentiate instruction. Of course, this can be done in terms of level because the instructor is able to help on a more individual basis as she or he circulates while students are working. However, it can also be done in terms of content. For example, if the class is mostly first-year college students or adults, some life-skills material may be of interest (and use) to them. Figure 30 presents a short reading and questions from *What Makes America Tick?* New college students or immigrants in an adult learning program might especially appreciate Expansion Activity 4 from the Instructor's Manual (see Figure 31). The analysis and pro/con lists can be completed in groups and presented in class.

In a flipped classroom, different instructors choose different content to present in class versus assign as homework. Expansion Activities in an Instructor's Manual allow for the incorporation of authentic materials that spur student interest and allow them to apply the knowledge beyond the ESL classroom. For example, in Expansion Activity 2 (see Figure 31) for *What Makes America Tick?* students can think about the questions they discussed and information from the reading to create their own city design. A formal or informal presentation can also be scheduled if desired so students can share the details of their interaction. This is nice if students eventually need to take a speech class or present in front of a professional audience. Expansion Activity 1 in Figure 31 helps students with more academic preparation and allows some reliance on personal experience if desired.

Figure 30. Example of Reading Content Ideal for Flipping a Culture Lesson

LINK TO TODAY: Credit Card Nation in Crisis—How Much Is Too Much?

Since World War II, consuming seems to be almost a matter of obligation in U.S. American society and cash has largely fallen out of fashion. It is nearly impossible to live and conduct business in the U.S without a credit card. Some popular credit cards in the United States are Visa, MasterCard, American Express, and Discover. In the United States, it is important to build a good credit history, which is measured by your **credit score**. This score can determine the interest rate on a bank loan or affect being hired for a job. Each person has three credit scores—Equifax, Experion, and Transunion—that are tied to a Social Security number. If you have a loan or credit card, it is a good idea to check your credit scores every year to make sure there is no false information and that you have not been a victim of identity theft. Generally speaking, a good credit score is 700 or above.

Until the 2007–2009 economic crisis, it was very easy to obtain a credit card. It was not uncommon to get multiple card offers in the mail or to be offered a gift such as a free product or t-shirt for filling out credit card applications on college campuses, at shopping malls, or in airports. This information was often sold to other marketing companies, who then advertised their products and services in the mail or over the phone (telemarketing). The recent economic downturn has resulted in a "credit crunch" that has made obtaining credit more difficult—especially for people with low credit scores or no credit history. The crisis has also made thrifty spending and cash payment fashionable again. One thing about life in the United States that does not change over time is that advertisers want money from consumers. It is a good idea to be careful about giving out personal information or buying things via mail, telephone, or the Internet, especially if you do not understand completely what is being offered. Many people, including native speakers, have been victims of illegal marketing scams.

Fast Facts

- The U.S. Congress passed the Credit Card Act in May 2009, with support from both major political parties in both the House of Representatives and the Senate. The law protects consumers against unfair or deceptive credit practices and restricts penalties, late charges, and interest rate hikes.
- The U.S. Federal Trade Commission gave a $1.13 million grant to the University of Missouri to conduct research into the fairness and efficiency with which credit score disputes are handled in support of the Fair Credit Reporting Act.
- A 2011 study by Pew Charitable Trusts found that credit card late payment fees decreased and interest rates stabilized as a result of the 2009 Credit CARD Act legislation.

- A U.S. Commerce Department report showed that consumer spending was down at the start of 2012 as compared to previous years.
- The U.S. Federal Reserve estimated in 2011 that consumer debt was more than $2.4 trillion at the end of 2011, with the average household having $6,500 in credit card debt in 2010.

Find and read two newspaper, magazine, or Internet articles, one with positive aspects of credit cards and one detailing the negative aspects. Summarize each article. Then write a short paragraph about your personal conclusions.

positive aspects of credit cards

_____

_____

_____

_____

negative aspects of credit cards

_____

_____

_____

_____

my personal conclusion(s) about credit cards in the United States

_____

_____

_____

_____

From: Ashby. (2012). *What Makes America Tick? 2nd Edition,* pages 64–65, University of Michigan Press.

Figure 31. Example of Activity Ideal for Flipped Culture Lesson

Expansion Activities

1. Ask students to write a report or create a presentation about their favorite artist or museum.
2. Group students and tell them to imagine they are a team of suburban developers commissioned to design a suburb outside the nearest city. Prepare them to present their design and the suburb features to the rest of the class.
3. Franklin Delano Roosevelt is considered by many to be one of the greatest presidents. Ask students to research his political career and create a timeline of events and decisions that helped shape his presidency. If desired, students can choose other presidents.
4. Bring in sample credit card offers. Ask students to choose one to analyze and write about the pros and cons to the offer.

From: Instructor's Manual to accompany *What Makes America Tick? 2nd Edition* (2012).

University or Academic Content

A big part of many academic programs is teaching students paraphrasing and summarizing to avoid plagiarism. Depending on their native culture, plagiarism might be a very new concept and students aren't often familiar with the seriousness or penalties. This type of content is easy to flip and is ideal for preparing students for academic settings, for use with authentic materials, and for research (group or individual). Figure 32 presents a box about source citations and about sorting sources from *Choice and Consequence: A Critical Reading Text*. Often, this material is presented in class and students are sent home to complete the online Sorting Sources chart (shown in Figure 33).

Flipping content or sources allows the opportunity for instructors to supply copies of the institution or department's handbook on citing (or let students refer to the citing guidelines for their fields or fields of interest) and/or bring copies of the institution's plagiarism policy and guidelines. Instructors can also conduct the academic springboard activity in class (see Figure 34) and then ask students to bring their Sorting Sources chart to class because studying the Citing Sources box and Sorting Sources information has already been done as homework.

Figure 32. Example of Writing Content Ideal for Flipped Writing Lesson

Citing Sources

The source of a published piece of work is also known as its **citation.** The readings in this text are followed by source citations to remind you that when you use information from them in your own writing, you must cite the original source. Professional and academic writers follow certain guidelines when they cite sources. When assigned to write an essay that includes quotes and/or paraphrases from one or more articles to support your own point of view on the topic, you will need to include both parenthetical references in the body of your paper and a full citation (a list of sources) at the end of your essay. Citing outside sources shows the reader that you have researched the topic and are thus knowledgeable about the subject matter, and that data, ideas, or facts included in an essay have been taken from credible sources. This protects you from committing plagiarism, which means using work from another author or group of writers without giving credit. Citations also show that opinions you have included are from experts in the field, permit you to include relevant material to support your own ideas, and enable readers to do further reading and research by finding the original work for themselves.

There are several formats for citing sources. Which format you will use is generally dictated by the academic discipline. Two of the most common formats are MLA (Modern Language Association) and APA (American Psychological Association). Using a standard format helps everyone understand the citations. The full citations for this online article are shown here in both APA and MLA formats. Examine each labeled component of the citations. It is very important to learn to write end-of-text references correctly for your assignments.

An APA end-of-text citation is placed on a new page at the end of the paper called *References.* The list of references is ordered alphabetically by authors' last names.

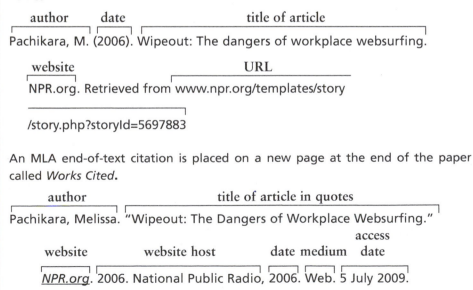

An MLA end-of-text citation is placed on a new page at the end of the paper called *Works Cited.*

Sorting Sources

When you read widely on a controversial topic, you will find that some texts are more objective than others. Authors who are objective try hard to report facts and a variety of perspectives on an issue, but they remain neutral themselves. Other writers express their opinions; they choose material carefully to support their views and hope to persuade readers to agree with them. Either way, you should keep notes on what you read in order to use material appropriately in your own writing.

When reading and analyzing information from a variety of sources, ask yourself questions about the authors' views. What are the main points, and how are they supported? Are there mostly facts or opinions? Who agrees with whom and why? Who presents an opposing viewpoint and why? Whose arguments are the most sound? A reading log can help you take note of this kind of information and prepare for a research-based essay. The companion website for this textbook contains a Sorting Sources Chart you can use to log information about each reading. Save the file, and add to it after each reading.

From: Tunceren & Benson. (2010). *Choice and Consequence,* pages 8–9, University of Michigan Press.

Figure 33. Example of Writing Content for Flipped Lesson

Chapter 1: Websurfing in the Workplace

	Author(s), title, source	Main purpose of article	Main ideas, claims of authors	Supporting details, examples	Quotes maybe to use in my essay
Reading 1					
Reading 2					
Reading 3					
Reading 4					
Reading 5					

From: Instructor's Manual to accompany *Choice and Consequence* (2010).

Figure 34. Example of Springboard Activity from an Instructor's Manual
ACADEMIC SPRINGBOARD
Supplement with your school's handbook as necessary. Depending on the class population, consider asking students to learn about the citation style used in their fields. Other styles include CMOS (Chicago Manual of Style), ACS (American Chemical Society), CBE (Council of Biology Editors), IEEE (Institute of Electrical and Electronics Engineering), NLM (National Library of Medicine), AAA (American Anthropological Association), and APSA (American Political Science Association).   This item represents a good opportunity for the class to review or study your institution's plagiarism policy and its punishments if broken. Bring copies or show the policy online for discussion in class.

From: Instructor's Manual to accompany *Choice and Consequence* (2010).

Other Authentic Material

Vocabulary textbooks and classes are often filled with a variety of words and activities designed to help students use words in context. *Vocabulary Mastery 3*, for example, contains sentence completion, matching, word part activities, defining, synonym practice, readings, and word charts, to name but a few. Much of the instruction in a traditional model class is done in class. Words are presented and defined, questions are answered, and a variety of activities are completed. As always, this model works. Students get ample vocabulary practice; however, a flipped model might allow students more opportunity to use the words in other contexts as well as make the class more interactive. If students learn the words on their own at home in their own time and do certain comprehension activities at home, then class time is available for critical thinking, discussion, and use of authentic materials. Instructors may have their own ideas, but the appendix of *Vocabulary Mastery 3* has some good ideas that may inspire new ideas for other classes. For the unit on Watergate, for example, two ideas that may spark inspiration are provided in Figure 35.

Figure 35. Examples of Activities to Inspire Use of Authentic Materials

Watergate

1. The Watergate scandal began with five men breaking into the Democratic National Committee headquarters in Washington, DC, and ended with the resignation of President Richard Nixon. If this happened today, do you think it would end the same way? What might be different?

2. Political cartoons are used by newspaper and magazine editorial cartoonists to send messages to the readers. See the example on page 42. They often use symbolism and exaggeration, among other techniques, to get their point across. Search the Internet for political cartoons published during and after the Watergate scandal. Share examples with the rest of the class.

Journalism

1. Read *All the President's Men* or watch the film. Talk about how the events depicted affected journalism.

2. During the Watergate years and for many years later, Woodward and Bernstein never revealed who Deep Throat was. Research the laws associated with reporters not revealing sources. Find a story about another journalist who has not revealed his or her source, the circumstances, and any punishments he or she faced.

3. Bring in a political cartoon from a recent newspaper. Prepare to discuss what event or person the cartoon is editorializing.

4. Look at a copy of the school, city, or national newspaper. Which section of the paper do you like to read most? What kind of stories would you like to write if you were a journalist? Talk about your choices with a small group.

From: Valcourt & Wells. (2010). *Vocabulary Mastery 3*, pages 183–184. University of Michigan Press.

Flipping with Technology

I Want to Use Audio, but I Don't Want To Be the "Star"

Of course, the most frequent component associated with flipped classrooms is the video. Although not required, it is often used by instructors in a variety of disciplines. This can be done in ESL as well. A lot of instructors don't want to make their own videos, whether that be because they don't want to create their own content or because they simply don't want to be on video. To incorporate video, instructors don't have to be the star. To best try this type of flipping, a good way is to apply the flipped model to a listening class. The recordings have already been taped, and so this is obviously what instructors would ask students to listen to outside of class. This audio component allows instructors to then replace whatever time had been reserved for playing audio and any replaying of the audio with "homework" or some project, discussion, or activity done in class.

A challenge many students seem to face is that of listening to lectures with visual aids. They tend to only write what is on the slide rather than listening to additional information. When teaching this strategy, it seems obvious that presenting the box on visual aids, playing the audio, and having students take notes and complete the short comprehension activities is the best strategy. Of course it works, but instructors may not have time to complete the activities that allow for further application of the content and more interactive discussion. However, if students listen and take notes as homework, then there is more class time for application, critical thinking, and discussion. Figure 36 illustrates an example of this strategy and shows one part of the note-taking task that could be done outside of class; it also shows an activity that can be done without time constraints if a flipped model is employed. See also Figure 37 for an example of a discussion activity. These activities are from *Four Point Listening and Speaking 1*.

Some books have full-length lectures and longer excerpts, and these are ideally suited for a flipped classroom setting for two reasons. First, they require a lot of time to listen to, and second, they best prepare students who intend to pursue a degree at an English-speaking institution. *Academic Listening Strategies* has longer listening passages. With the listening excerpts from this text ranging from just a couple of minutes to 30 minutes all the way up to 50 minutes, listening outside of class is ideal. Students can spend more time listening and often do, which in turn results in more practice and increased comprehension in general.

Figure 36. Example of Listening/Note-Taking Content for Flipping

Strategy: Taking Notes on Visual Aids

Many instructors use a chalk or whiteboard or electronic slides during their lectures. Often, the information on the board or slide contains the headings or main points and some general information. The lecture will contain more details, but you can use the headings and general information as a guide to help you figure out what to include in your notes.

Listening to a Lecture

[Exercise not shown in full.]

The listening passage is a lecture from a business class. The instructor is discussing a tool some businesses use when trying to develop a new product or that entrepreneurs use to analyze a new company. Use the headings on the slides to organize your notes as you listen to the lecture on SWOT analyses. Write your notes next to the slide that would be shown when the instructor is giving the details.

Slide 1

A SWOT Analysis
Definitions, Examples, Template

_____

_____

_____

_____

_____

Slide 2

Strengths—Definition

_____

_____

_____

_____

_____

Creating a SWOT Analysis

Work with your entrepreneurial team. Create a SWOT analysis for the business you created. Present your analysis to the class.

From: Folse & Lockwood. (2010). *Four Point Listening and Speaking 1*, pages 100, 104, 110, University of Michigan Press.

Figure 37. Example of Discussion Activity to Flip

Discussion

The students in the video discuss new business ideas for a restaurant, bookstore, article of clothing, and a school supply. Work with a group to develop one of those four ideas. You can continue to develop one of their ideas or create a new twist on one of their ideas. Take notes about your business, and be prepared to present your business to the class.

Product or Idea: _____

Audience: _____

Who is our competition?

_____

_____

_____

What is special about our product or idea?

_____

_____

_____

What are our goals?

_____

_____

_____

How will we achieve our goals? What are our strategies to get customers?

_____

_____

_____

From: Folse & Lockwood. (2010). *Four Point Listening and Speaking 1*, page 95, University of Michigan Press.

Don't forget that the instructor's manual might also have ideas for more outside the class work, authentic materials, and/or in-class projects (see Figure 38).

Figure 38. Example of Activity from an Instructor's Manual to Flip

Expansion Activity

Print a copy of the audio script. Ask students to review the textbook and note what main ideas they would put on a slide and what information they think they would have to put in their notes. Point out that in many cases, the lecturers put main ideas, but give examples and details while the slide is showing. Encourage students to look at professors' websites or the course management system to see if the slides are available before or after the lecture. If they're available before, encourage students to use the print mode shown in this textbook to take notes in class. If they're available later, remind them that it's okay to write what they can and organize using the print mode later.

Consider using an authentic lecture and slides. The University of Notre Dame has a medical ethics course online with audio and slides available at http://ocw.nd.edu/philosophy/medical-ethics/lectures-1/lectures. Give students a copy of the PPT in advance and then play the audio for them to practice taking notes on material not included on the slides.

Also consider asking a colleague in another class for slides to use as an example, especially if the lecture is recorded.

From: Instructor's Manual to accompany *Four Point Listening and Speaking 1* (2010).

Letting Someone Else Be the "Star"

Guest Speakers

Guest speakers have proven to be a good way to flip, and they are useful in providing a wide variety of different content. For example, when studying question format or determining a speaker's purpose, instructors can invite a guest speaker. Students plan questions or later discuss the speaker's purpose. Often, other departments or offices on campus (like Campus Safety or Career Development) are very happy to send someone to speak about the offices' services. Students can then ask questions to the speaker or have discussions about the content after the speaker closes. This builds both listening and speaking skills without the teacher being the "sage on the stage." Often the speakers bring their own authentic materials or activities for the students, leading to interaction that typifies the flipped model approach and saves the instructor a lot of work beyond simply scheduling the speaker to come in.

Some textbooks also have material that either prepares students for a future guest speaker or that can be used in lieu of a guest speaker. The example from *Academic Listening Strategies* shows a task related to a guest speaker from a Campus Safety office that is available on one of the DVDs that accompany the textbook (see Figure 39). If desired, this activity can be completely done at home with a short discussion in class for comparison and sharing of answers. Then students can listen to a guest speaker from the school's campus safety department. Schedule time for Q&A or an activity related to the textbook content or realia. If a speaker can't be brought to class, then consider taking the class to the guest speaker. Field trips to museums or visits to campus offices can often be arranged.

Figure 39. Example of Listening Activity Followed by a Guest Speaker

TASK 29

This final exercise will help you focus on several of the features of spoken English and strategies for listening that you have learned about in this unit. Listen to a short talk given by Officer Mathews on campus safety. The strategies you should use are *predicting and using background knowledge; listening for headings; and listening to word-level stress, pauses, and redundancy.*

STEP 1

Discuss with a classmate what you can do to learn about campus crime and what you can do to be safe on your campus. Then look up information about campus safety on the Internet. After you find information, discuss the results. Make some predictions about the talk and what you think you will hear.

STEP 2

Listen to the clip and take notes in the space provided.

_____

_____

_____

_____

STEP 3

Answer these questions:

1. What is the most common crime on campus?

   _____

2. How can it be avoided?

   _____

3. Describe how this type of crime commonly happens.

   _____

4. What items are commonly stolen?

   _____

5. What other safety tips are given with regard to serial numbers, ATM machines, and walking at night?

_____

_____

_____

_____

_____

STEP 4

Officer Mathews's talk has some features of an information talk (an open style). Some of the features of this talk that convey informality are:

• the setting: a small classroom, not a large lecture hall

• conversational style

• slang: *computers are a very hot ticket item to steal; that's a big no no*

• linking and reduction: *it's better to do that than ta hafta try ta borrow notes from somebody; they're gonna probably want some o that money*

• addressing the audience as *you*

STEP 5

Officer Mathews gives some direct advice in this talk. He uses command forms here:

> *Do not leave any of your property unattended for any amount of time.*

> *Secure your property at all times and it means all times.*

> *Make sure that every thing you have that you can't live without is with you at all times.*

Why do you think he is so direct? What is the purpose of this talk?

_____

_____

_____

_____

STEP 6

Notice the redundancy present in Officer Mathews's talk. Why do you think he repeated himself so much?

_____

STEP 7

1. Does the information that Officer Mathews gave surprise you in any way?

_____

_____

2. What kinds of crimes are typical on the campuses that you are familiar with?

_____

_____

From: Salehzadeh. (2005). *Academic Listening Strategies*, pages 70–72, University of Michigan Press.

Contact Activities—Strangers Can Be the "Stars"

For me, flipping writing was the easiest. Looking at it very simply, I asked students to do the book work at home and then write in class. There's more to it, of course, but that seemed to be the easiest way for me to grasp the idea and try to implement it. Flipping my listening class proved easy enough since video and audio existed, either with my textbooks or from the wealth of audio and visual available online. The speaking class was harder to flip though. Isn't a speaking class already flipped since the students talk a lot? Can it be flipped more? Can we extend speaking beyond short dialogues and role-plays?

One of the tenets of a flipped classroom is having the instructor not be "sage on the stage" and be more of a "guide on the side." If this is to happen, students need to talk to someone other than the instructor and even to others who are not peers in the classroom. They need to experience content beyond staged dialogues. It's possible that homework involves students talking to people outside of the classroom. Contact activities attempt to prompt students to speak to others besides classmates. This type of contact activity is often assigned as homework after practicing in class or is skipped altogether. When done, it can be collected or discussed in class. However, why not flip this activity and let students use class time?

Figure 40 from the *Four Point* series shows a simple presentation on greetings, a related practice activity, and a Making Contact activity often assigned as homework.

Students might say they didn't have time to complete this activity regardless of how little time it would take or even the fact that they could complete it while they were in other classes. Instructors might also find that some students have confidence issues. Students may simply not be confident enough to do it on their own. By flipping this type of activity, instructors can send students out during class time for 15 minutes to complete the chart and then discuss the answers right away in class. To build confidence, students could work in pairs to complete the chart. This is also a great way to provide time for students to get up and move around; it breaks up the tedium of the class before proceeding with more content. See also Figure 41.

Figure 40. Example of Speaking Content to Flip a Multi-Level Lesson

Greetings

Before starting a conversation or discussion, most people begin with a greeting. This sometimes breaks the ice and helps the interaction seem friendly and open. There are many greetings in English, and some are more formal than others.

Using Greetings

Think about greetings, and answer these questions with a partner. Then share your ideas with the class.

1. Would you greet each of these people formally or informally?

   a. your English teacher _____

   b. an instructor in your department _____

   c. the department chairperson _____

   d. your roommate _____

   e. a relative _____

   f. a cashier at the bookstore _____

   g. a new classmate who sits next to you in class _____ _____

Formal	Informal
Hello.	Hi.
Good morning/afternoon/evening.	Hey.
How are you?	How you doing?
It's nice to see you.	What's up?
It's been a long time.	Long time, no see.
How have you been?	How's it going?
How are things going?	What's new?

2. What greetings do you frequently use every day? Add other greetings to the list.

_____

_____

3. What things affect the greeting and/or the response? Does the place or time of the interaction matter? Does the formality of the greeting affect the response?

_____

_____

Making Contact

Choose three greetings from the list and greet three different English speakers. Take notes on the greeting you used, the response you received, and the details of the interaction (person's status, age, and gender, the time of day, and the location). Follow the example. Be prepared to discuss your data with the class.

Your Greeting	The Person's Response	Details of the Interaction
Hi.	Hi.	classmates, same age, male, morning, hallway

From: Folse & Lockwood. (2011). *Four Point Listening and Speaking Intro*, pages 8–9, University of Michigan Press.

Figure 41. Example of a Multi-Level Lesson from an Instructor's Manual
Expansion Activity
Have students compare their answers with information found in MICASE (the Michigan Corpus of Academic English) or another corpus. Ask students questions such as *How are the greetings you found the same as those in the corpus? Different? What explanations might explain those similarities or differences? Were there any new words or phrases that could be added to the list?* For more information on MICASE, read the appendix in *Four Point Listening and Speaking* 1 or the information on the MICASE website at www.elicorpora.info/.

From: Instructor's Manual to accompany *Four Point Listening and Speaking Intro* (2011).

Using Scripts—One Way for Students To Be the "Stars"

Most listening and speaking textbooks, and even online sources, have scripts provided with recorded material. Many of my students actually enjoyed working with the scripts, far more than I expected, and it worked especially well when they worked in groups. Students can perform the script, record their own, or analyze and rewrite scripts. Instructors can videorecord any performances, and both students and instructor can use recordings for evaluative purposes.

As mentioned earlier, speaking activities in class seem as though they're already flipped, or at least "semi-flipped." They're interactive, done in class, and apply the material. However, some ideas allow for further flipping and better prepare students for discussions beyond the ESL classroom.

In a more traditional classroom, instructors present words and phrases in the speaking boxes and play the audio or video content. Questions are answered. Students then participate in an activity if time allows. But here's how I flipped content from the *Four Point* series in my class. Students studied the listening strategy and speaking strategy (see Figures 42 and 43) and then I played the video (available online at www.press.umich.edu/elt/compsite/4Point/LSintro videos). Students then formed groups to answer the questions (see Figure 44). If time allowed, I paired students to apply the information using the Information Gap activity (see Figure 45). Note that instructor's manuals often include other ideas for using scripts (see Figure 45).

Figure 42. Example of Listening Content to Flip an EAP Lesson

Strategy: Listening for and Using Spatial Signal Words and Phrases

Some academic discussions and lectures describe a place or an illustration. To give you a mental picture or help you find something in a physical picture, speakers will use spatial words or phrases to guide the listeners. There are many words and phrases that describe where something is.

Spatial Signal Words and Phrases

above	close (to)
across (from)	far (from)
adjacent (to)	in
after	inside
at	near
behind	next to
below	on
beside	outside
between	to the left (of)
by	to the right (of)
centered	under

More than one spatial word or phrase can be used in a sentence.

Neon is **in** the row **below** helium.

Cobalt is **near** nickel and **centered** in the fourth row.

Many spatial words and phrases are used as part of prepositional phrases.

Hydrogen is **at the top** of the periodic table.

Neon is **in the row** below helium.

Pronunciation Note: In prepositional phrases, the object of the preposition receives the main stress. As a speaker, you need to decide how important the spatial word is. If you use it as part of a prepositional phrase (as in *in the row*), you will not stress it. Therefore, you need to listen carefully for spatial signals.

Nickel is in the fourth **ROW not** Neon is **IN** the fourth row.

From: Folse & Lockwood. (2011). *Four Point Listening and Speaking Intro*, page 139, University of Michigan Press.

Figure 43. Example of Speaking Content for Flipped EAP Lesson

CONFIRMING CORRECT OR INCORRECT

Correct	Incorrect
Yes. / Yep.	No.
That's right.	No, sorry, that's not right.
Right.	Nope. That's not it.
Exactly.	Close, but not exactly. Sort of, but not exactly. Kind of, but not exactly.
Yes, correct.	Sorry.
Perfect.	Not exactly, no.
Okay.	Nope.
You've got it.	Unfortunately, that's not right.

From: Folse & Lockwood. (2011). *Four Point Listening and Speaking Intro,* page 141, University of Michigan Press.

Figure 44. Example of Video Questions for a Flipped EAP Lesson

Focus on Language

1. What words or phrases do the students use when they give an opinion?
   Note: Refer to the box. Don't worry about writing exact words.

   _____

   _____

2. Do any students ask for an explanation? What words do they use? Refer to the box. Note: Don't worry about writing exact words.

   _____

   _____

3. Where are the elements they talk about on the periodic table?

_____

_____

4. What confirmations for correct or incorrect are used? <u>Note</u>: Don't worry about writing exact words.

_____

_____

5. Write any phrases or idioms that you are not familiar with. Discuss what they mean and in what type of interactions they are appropriate.

_____

_____

Focus on Tone

1. Who do you think uses the best tone of voice? Why do you like this person's tone best?

_____

_____

2. Is each person's tone appropriate? Why or why not?

_____

_____

3. List the prepositional phrases you hear. Which words are stressed most in the phrases?

_____

_____

Focus on Nonverbal Communication

1. What nonverbal cues are used to show how each person feels during the discussion?

_____

_____

2. Was any nonverbal communication inappropriate? Why or why not?

_____

_____

3. Which student do you think has the most expressive facial expressions? Is this good or bad for the interaction?

_____

_____

Summary

1. Which student does a better job of using spatial words and phrases? Give a reason for your opinion.

_____

_____

_____

_____

2. Which student uses the best combination of words, tone, and nonverbal communication? Support your answer.

_____

_____

_____

_____

3. Who would you most want to work with? Why? Who would you rather not work with? Why?

_____

_____

_____

_____

From: Folse & Lockwood. (2011). *Four Point Listening and Speaking Intro,* pages 143–146, University of Michigan Press.

Figure 45. Example of an Information Gap Activity Ideal for Flipping

Information Gap

The chemical elements are organized into the Periodic Table. The elements are arranged from left to right and top to bottom. They are in order from the lowest to the highest atomic number.

Work with a partner to complete the missing information about the elements in the chart in the first three columns. Complete the last column of the chart together by finding the element in the current periodic table and describing its location using spatial signals. Confirm correct and incorrect as needed. When you're finished, a sample row would look like this:

Atomic Number	Symbol	Name	Location
21	Sc	Scandium	fourth row, third from the left

Atomic Number	Symbol	Name	Location
1	H	Hydrogen	
6	C		
	Na	Sodium	
14		Silicon	
	Ti	Titanium	
29	Cu		
	Ag		
50		Tin	
79		Gold	
80	Hg		
	Rn	Radon	
88	Ra	Radium	

Atomic Number	Symbol	Name	Location
1	H	Hydrogen	
6		Carbon	
11	Na		
	Si	Silicon	
22	Ti		
29		Copper	
47		Silver	
50		Tin	
79	Au		
80	Hg	Mercury	
86			
	Ra	Radium	

From: Folse & Lockwood. (2011). *Four Point Listening and Speaking Intro,* pages 147–148, University of Michigan Press.

Figure 46. Example of Activity from Instructor's Manual for a Flipped EAP Class

Expansion Activity

Photocopy the script that is available at www.press.umich.edu/elt/tm/ and have students perform it. They can perform it as it is and then compare themselves to the video clip. Or, ask them to change the language, nonverbal cues, and tone and perform it again. Ask them to explain their changes and the reasons for them. Consider recording them and scheduling individual meetings to talk about the differences and their own strengths and weaknesses.

From: Instructor's Manual to accompany *Four Point Listening and Speaking Intro* (2011).

To further the flipped model using videos and scripts, students study the strategies on their own at home and complete any associated practice activities. They also watch the video at home, take notes, and complete the questions (see Figure 44). In class, they discuss their answers to the questions and complete the Information Gap activity (because now there is time for this since more is done at home). Additionally, there might even be time for an activity using the script (see Figure 46). For example, students can mark the script by identifying the language used (confirming or correcting their answers to the Focus on Language section), edit the script to their liking, or perform it as is trying to best mimic natural language.

Using Existing Material and Videos

There are occasions when it's very nice for the material to be presented in some format other than accompanying text material. A lot of material already exists! Covering a unit on astronomy in your ESL text? Check the links for educators on the website for the National Aeronautics and Space Administration (NASA). Does your book cover weather or do you want to prepare students for a science lesson? Try the National Oceanic and Atmospheric Administration's (NOAA) education resources link. A lot of ESL books have units on current events. Look at the lesson plans available on the *New York Times* Learner's Network (learning.blogs.nytimes.com) and use the actual newspaper as authentic material. After all, students will likely read the news long after they finish their education.

There are a lot of videos out there that are free to use and can even accompany material in textbooks if desired. The box in Figure 47 from the *Four Point Reading and Writing Intro* textbook can be used with videos already prepared online. One video already prepared is called "Basics of Citing, MLA, 3 of 3" (In-Text Citation) on YouTube at www.youtube.com/watch?v=2xTL7mhPlr8. A quick YouTube search for whatever content being taught is likely to generate a video. Try it by conducting a keyword search for a grammar component; it will likely lead you to many, many videos.

For example, if you are using *Clear Grammar 4, 2nd Edition* (Folse), and the lesson is on the past perfect tense, searching for "past perfect tense" in the YouTube search bar will produce a list of many options available. Students can watch videos at home as well with any instruction from the text before completing activities in the classroom. Of course, using an online search engine and not just YouTube generates even more video clips and material already prepared about ESL content.

Figure 47. Example of Reading-Writing Content to Use with Videos

---

FYI: Understanding In-Text Citations and Bibliographic/Reference Entries

In some texts, in-text citations appear instead of bibliographic footnotes. See examples in Reading 2 like (Kendon, 1997). The citation in parentheses provides the name(s) of author(s) and year of publication. It only includes this brief information because the rest of the publication information appears at the end of the article or book in the Bibliography, list of Works Cited, or list of References, depending on the style (APA, MLA).

The entry usually includes the author(s), the title, the publisher, and year of publication, as shown at the end of Reading 2. If it's a book, the location of the publisher is also listed. If it's a magazine or journal article, the name of the publication is included with the volume number and/or issue number and page number.

If it's an online article, the name of the website and the web address are usually included.

From: Lockwood & Sippell. (2012). *Four Point Reading and Writing Intro*, page 97, University of Michigan Press.

Using Other Sites

To help students apply the skills and strategies learned in the ESL classroom, use the many available content lectures available online. To do this, students listen to the content or lecture outside of class and then participate in activities or projects during class. I use a lecture project activity in my listening class. It involves students preparing vocabulary, comprehension, and/or discussion activities for the other students. All students listen to the selected lectures outside of class and take notes. They use their notes to participate in the presentations for other lectures, but they also use them for their group project to plan the activities, discuss the content, and create their PowerPoint slides for the lecture their group will present on. This planning is what used to be "homework," but now they work with their group inside class where I can be available to help as needed.

Some good sites include:

Academic Earth: http://academicearth.org/

Free Video Lectures: http://freevideolectures.com/

Harvard Open Courses: Open Learning Initiative: http://www.extension.harvard.edu/open-learning-initiative Khan Academy: www.khanacadmy.org

Open Yale Courses: http://oyc.yale.edu/

Stanford University's Frederick H. Hillier Series: http://www.stanford.edu/dept/lc/efs/2013/summer/index.html. Some lectures from past years already have shorter clips provided, questions, and vocabulary. You can read the Teacher Resource Guide at www.stanford.edu/dept/lc/efs/TeacherResourceGuide.html.

Other sites (many of which have transcripts or educational tools):

CNN Student News: http://www.cnn.com/studentnews/ You can find transcripts, a daily curriculum, discussion questions, and maps for the daily program: http://www.cnn.com/2013/09/02/studentnews/sn-curriculum-tue/index.html.

NPR: www.npr.org

PBS. Click on the Teachers Link at www.pbs.org to find classroom-ready, digital resources and lesson plans.

TED: Ideas Worth Spreading: www.ted.com

TeacherTube: www.teachertube.com

Youtube: www.youtube.com

Youtube: Education: https://www.youtube.com/education

But I Want To Be the "Star"

Because some teachers want to film their own video or audio content, a few easy-to-use resources are listed. Some are free. Many sources say the videos should not be long and that those under 10 minutes work well.

Audacity: audacity.sourceforge.net

CamStudio: camstudio.org

Camtasia Studio: www.techsmith.comcamtasia.html

Jing: www.techsmith.com/jing.html

Panopto: www.panopto.com

Screencast: screencast.com

Screencast-o-matic: http://www.screencast-o-matic.com/

Screenr: www.screenr.com

Snagit: www.techsmith.com/snagit/html

Sophia: www.sophia.org

StudyMate: http://www.respondus.com/products/studymate/index.shtml

Tegrity: www.tegrity.com

VoiceThread: voicethread.com

YouTube: www.youtube.com

Consider starting by recording something short and simple or by video-taping your introduction to students on the first day of class. Encourage all the students to post their own introductions on whatever course management system is available.

Let Someone Else Create the Activities

Most publishers have online activities and resources available that can be used in a flipped classroom. There are also companion websites with a wealth of vocabulary activities and additional handouts or worksheets for students. Many publishers now offer online activities that can be used in class, or there are others that colleagues have posted or that are available by searching for the concept in an Internet search engine. Utilize test banks to create questions and quizzes for use as games or quizzes in class or as comprehension checks outside of class. Using these sources will allow a flipped classroom of sorts by having students participate in class rather than doing these as homework. Scheduling time in the school's computer lab or letting students complete activities in class (individually, in pairs, or in groups) are good ways to flip. Similarly, find books that explain how to set up activities, such as book clubs (*Creating Book Clubs in the English Language Classroom* by Vaille and QuinnWilliams) or corpus-based activities (*Using Corpora in the Language Learning Classroom* by Bennett). Look through teacher training catalogs to find resources that work best for you.

Conclusion

Flipping the classroom isn't necessarily new, depending on who you ask, and it still seems to be evolving. What that means for the ESL classroom has yet to be determined, but the degree to which you flip and when you flip is up to you. In general, flipping or starting to flip the ESL classroom doesn't have to be hard, and we in the ESL field have the chance and flexibility to make it work in the ways that are best for our students and best for us. It can be a gradual change as you determine what kind of classroom activities can be used with your students and textbooks, or you can go all in and implement the flipped approach with existing videos or by making your own videos. ESL teachers are lucky in that they can make this flipped approach what they need to best serve their objectives as teachers and give students what they need it to be successful. It's worth a try.

Why not try to flip just one lesson? Try it tomorrow! In time, this style of learning may not have a label and might just be the way we teach.

Sources and Additional Resources

Bergmann, Jonathan and Sams, Aaron. (2012). *Flip your classroom: Reach every student in every class every day.* Washington, D.C. International Society for Technology and Education.

Bergmann, Jon, Overmyer, Jerry, Wilie, Brett. The Daily Riff. (2013). *The flipped class: Myths vs. reality.* www.thedailyriff.com/articles/the-flipped-class-conversation-689.php.

Classroom Window. (2012). *Flipped classrooms: Improved test scores and teacher satisfaction.* Retrieved from http://classroomwindow.com/flipped-classrooms-improved-test-scores-and-teacher-satisfaction

Cockrum, Tony. (2014). *Flipping your English class to reach all learners: Strategies and lesson plans.* New York: Routledge.

Ferenstein, Gregory. (2013, September). The Flipped Classroom Boosts Grades 5%. Why That's As Big As We Can Expect. Tech Crunch. Retrieved from http://techcrunch.com/2013/09/18/the-flipped-classroom-boosts-grades-5-why-thats-as-big-as-we-can-expect/

Flipped Learning Network. Available at flippedlarning.org

Gerstein, Judy. (n.d.). *The flipped classroom.* Resources compiled at *www.scoop.it/t/the-flipped-classroom.*

Gifford, Danny. (2013, January 10). Flipped classroom gaining popularity among profs. *The Stanford Daily.* 2013, January 10.

Herreid, C.F., and Schiller, N.A. (2013). Case studies and the flipped classroom. *Journal of College Science Teaching, 42(5),* 62.

Hoag, Christina. (2013, January 27). Teachers Flip for "Flipped Learning" Class Model.

Available at http://bigstory.ap.org/article/teachers-flip-flipped-learning-class-model

Khan, Salman. (2012). *The one world schoolhouse: Education reimagined.* New York: Hatchette Book Group.

Learn Spark. (n.d.) Flipped Classroom. Available at http://learn-spark.blogspot.com/2012/09/flipped-classroom.html

Lytle, Alan D. (2013). Flipping the classroom. *HEIS News: The Newsletter of the Higher Education Interest Section.* TESOL

Marshall, Helaine. (2013). Three Reasons to Flip Your Classroom. *Bilingual Basics: The Newsletter of the Bilingual Interest Section and Teachers of English to Deaf Students.* TESOL.

Meyer, Robinson. (2013, September 13). The post-lecture classroom: How will students fare? *The Atlantic.* http://www.theatlantic.com/technology/archive/2013/09/the-post-lecture-classroom-how-will-students-fare/279663/

Overmyer, Jerry (2013). The Flipped Learning Network. Flippedclassroom.org.

Ray-Treviño, S. (2013). Changing the focus to 21st century skills: One educator's experience. *The Language Educator, 8*(3), 22–23.

Wills, C. (2012). *Flipped classroom*. Retrieved from http://learn-spark.blogspot.com/2012/09/flipped-classroom.html

University of Michigan Press Textbooks/Resources Featured in *Flip It!*

Academic Listening Strategies: A Guide to Understanding Lectures, Julia Saleh-zadeh, 2005 (available packaged with or without the DVDs)

Academic Writing for Graduate Students: Essential Tasks and Skills, 3rd Edition, John Swales & Christine B. Feak, 2012

Challenges 1: Reading and Vocabulary for Academic Success, Cynthia Boardman & Laurie Barton, 2012

Choice and Consequence: A Critical Reading Text, Li-Lee Tunceren & Susan Benson, 2010

Clear Grammar 2: Keys to Grammar for English Language Learners, 2nd Edition, Keith S. Folse, 2012

Four Point Listening and Speaking Intro (EAP), Keith S. Folse & Robyn Brinks Lockwood, 2011

Four Point Listening and Speaking 1 (EAP), Keith S. Folse & Robyn Brinks Lockwood, 2010

Four Point Reading and Writing Intro (EAP), Robyn Brinks Lockwood & Kelly Sippell, 2012

Inside Academic Writing: Understanding Audience and Becoming Part of an Academic Community, Grace Canseco, 2010

Reader's Choice, 5th Edition, Sandra Silberstein, Mark A. Clarke, & Barbara K. Dobson, 2008

Taking Sides: Speaking Skills for College Students, Second Edition, Kevin B. King, 2008

Thinking Critically: World Issues for Reading, Writing, and Research, Second Edition, Myra Shulman, 2014

Vocabulary Mastery 1: Using and Learning the Academic Word List, Wells, 2007

Vocabulary Mastery 3: Using and Learning the Academic Word List, Linda Wells & Gladys Valcourt, 2010

What Makes America Tick? A Multiskill Approach to English through U.S. Culture and History, Second Edition, Wendy Ashby, 2012

What's Up 3: Integrated Skills and Culture for Adults, Kathleen Olson, 2009

Any Instructor's Manuals referenced in this book can be found online at www.press.umich.edu/elt/tm/. For more information about any of these books, go to www.press.umich.edu/elt/. To request examination copies, please use the online form at www.press.umich.edu/elt/examform.

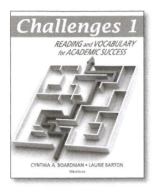
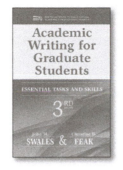
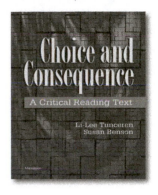

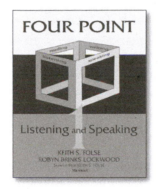
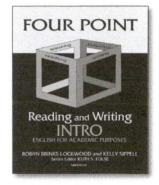
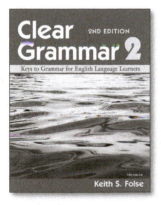
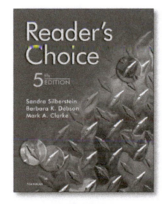
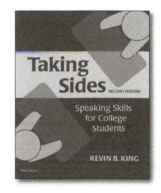

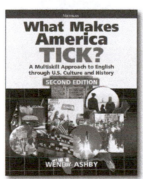
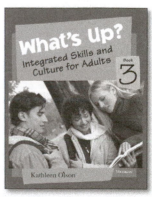